B+
7.75

A
HISTORY OF HUNGARY
IN BIOGRAPHICAL SKETCHES

CONTENTS

1*

PRINCE ÁRPÁD.

(† 907.)

*The monument of Árpád the Leader in Budapest. The an-
cestral settlement. Lebedia. Etelköz. Confederation of the
seven tribes. Árpád elected Leader. Hungaro-Bulgarian war.
The Nation's new home. The settlement. Árpád's work of
organization. His death.*

At the far end of the Andrássy-út, the most handsome
thoroughfare in Budapest, stands the Millenary column.
It was raised to commemorate the occupation of the
country by our Magyar ancestors a thousand year ago.
The column is surmounted by an angel, slim and tall, who
announces to the world in the words of the great national
poet that although diminished in number, the nation is
still unbroken in spirit after centuries of vicissitudes and
struggle. Round the base of the monument are several
equestrian statues — the splendid creations of George
Zala's genius — representing some of the Hungarian
leaders, who conquered the country. The central figure,
resting his right hand on his club, gazes earnestly, almost
sternly, into the distance before him, as if to read the future
destiny of the people whom, after untold hardship and
many a battle, he has led to the banks of the Danube.
Obviously not merely ambitious, but also able to command,
we cannot but feel that Prince Árpád deserves the respect
and homage even of his remotest descendents. Of his

person and subsequent exploits little is known. The history of his rule was not recorded by his contemporaries, or possibly, if any of the Hungarian Druids acquainted with the art of writing did leave records of it, they have been lost in the ensuing ages. Traditional lore, handed down by word of mouth from generation to generation, has kept alive the memory of his arresting personality and of the great achievement that made his name famous — the occupation of Hungary by the Hungarians.

The full significance of that historic event and the prominent part played in it by Prince Árpád will be best understood if we cast a glance into the history of the Hungarians — or Magyars as they are called in their own language — previous to it.

Their original home was probably somewhere on the western boundary of Southern Siberia, though we do not know exactly where it was situated. The total number of Hungarians at that time did not exceed that of the Hungarian prisoners in Siberia during the world war. In course of time this small nation split into two bodies, and the smaller of the two migrated westward. Today we can give no reason for this separation. Was it over-population that made co-existence difficult, or did internal feuds compel the vanquished to flee? Or was material adversity responsible for the exodus? Who today can tell?

In their westward migration the Hungarians had to battle their way along a route best by danger. They were few in number, for even some decades later, when they had been joined by other tribes, their total strength did not amount to the present population of Oxford and Cambridge. The lowlands north and west of the Caspian Sea, where they settled after leaving their original home, did not lend themselves to defence, and they lived in constant danger from surprise attacks. The migrating Hungarians presented the appearance of a band of nomads, but one whose line of march had been well explored, and only when the surrounding terrain had been thoroughly reconnoitred did they pitch their tents — usually in grazing ground. They subsisted, like other nomadic tribes, mainly on their flocks and herds, fishing and the chase. Small bands, or even tribes, of men mounted on swift horses assembled from time to time and set forth on expeditions into far-distant regions, to spy out their populations and wealth, and to ascertain that no danger threatened their own camps. Thus their reputation as a stern, disciplined and warlike people had already preceded them when they arrived on the northern shores of the Black Sea. This newly acquired territory was named Lebedia after Lebed, who was the greatest chieftain during their migrations. Lebed, though chief of but one tribe, was by universal consent acknowledged leader by all the tribes throughout their wanderings. In course of time the number of these tribes had increased to seven. These went by the names of Nyék, Magyar, Kürtgyarmat, Tarján, Jenő, Kara, and Kaza. It had ever been their custom to invest one of the chieftains with supreme leadership — this being imperative to maintain order and discipline — who was obeyed without question during their migrations. His authority, however, came to an end the moment they settled down. However, when they came to live in Lebedia, and a little later in Etelköz, now called Bessarabia, the chiefs of the seven tribes, prompted by experience, decided to make the paramount chieftainship permanent, i. e. the leader or prince continued to rule even after they

7

had settled and were living in peace. They had come to realize that divided leadership did not conduce to prosperity, for during their wanderings they saw that those families, or tribes, which were governed by one experienced, energetic, and just man prospered and were respected, and they came to the conclusion that if all seven tribes were under the permanent authority of one such man, the importance and strength of the Hungarians would not fail to increase. They soon acted on this wise resolve by choosing Lebed as leader. Although this was a universal choice, their old commander declined the great honour, feeling that it required a strong hand and a keen mind to govern. He recommended either Álmos, chieftain of the Magyar tribe, or Árpád, the valiant son of Álmos. And thus it came that Árpád was duly installed in his high position by being raised on a shield, according to the ancient custom. This meant that the tribes, which during their migrations had been but loosely held together, were now welded into one people, thereafter known to history as the Hungarian Nation. This union was by no means an unimportant matter, since it attracted the attention of the Greek Emperor, who began to take a greater interest in these Turk-like people — actually called "Turks" by the Greeks — who had made their appearance on the frontiers of the Empire and had just elected to themselves a Prince. Shrewd Greek merchants, under the Emperor's instructions and no doubt also attracted by prospects of trade, visited the Hungarians in Etelköz, and reported Árpád, the Prince of the Hungarians, to be "a man wise in mind and council, eminently valiant and qualified for government," also a strict disciplinarian supported by a brave and numerous army, with whom therefore it would be wise to establish friendly relations.

This report of the merchants was anything but welcome in the Greek metropolis, already seriously alarmed by the spread of the rising Bulgar Empire, the boundaries of which had been extended to include not only the Bulgaria of today, but also — with the exception of the northern and north-western parts — what later was to be known as Hungary. Now it seemed that besides these Turco-Bulgars, another race of the same stock was about to settle on the frontiers of the Byzantine Empire. Etelköz, bounded by rivers on the east and south and on the west by trackless wooded uplands, promised to be an extremely suitable domain for the Hungarians, and the possibility of these two peoples of kindred race eventually forming an alliance and founding a mighty Empire was a menace fraught with the uttermost peril to Byzantium. The Greeks already forsaw the country peopled with hordes of Hungarians and Bulgars, plundering and laying waste the towns and villages and destroying the fruits of Greek civilization. To avert this threatened danger Byzantium resorted to the policy of setting the two kindred races against each other. Whichever conquered would mean only one foe would threaten the Greek frontiers. The ruse was successful. On various pretexts and with tempting promises they induced the Hungarians to make war on the Bulgars. In the ensuing battles Prince Árpád's warriors won such decisive victories and the Bulgars sustained such crushing defeats that the Empire of the latter was broken and the goal of Byzantine policy achieved: there was one enemy less on the frontiers of the Greek Empire.

But victory cost the Hungarians more than it was worth. The Bulgars did not forget their defeat, and aware that unaided they were no match for the Hungarians, cast about for allies. One such they found in the warlike Petcheneggs, hereditary foes of the Hungarians, who at this time were living in Lebedia. They readily joined the Bulgars, and the Hungarians, attacked on two fronts in Etelköz, were defeated after a fierce struggle (895 A. D.). This defeat taught the Hungarians a salutary lesson. The report of the Greek merchants about the wisdom of Prince Árpád was not a gratuitous assumption. He could take a warning when it presented itself and quickly realized that his people dare not remain in Etelköz, since it was threatened on two sides by enemies who could always repeat their invasions and whose numerical superiority would render resistance vain. The question, then, was to find a country easily defended against invasion in time of war and affording the possibilities of prosperous settlement in time of peace. After lengthy consideration Árpád decided to lead his people across the mountain ranges (the Carpathians) on the border of Etelköz and settle with them on suitable territory on the far side. His choice fell upon what is now known as Hungary, which ever since — for more than a thousand years — has been the home of the Hungarians. Árpád was not guided in his choice by chance. It had happened that one or other of the more venturesome and unruly tribes made raids which took them great distances from the settlement in Etelköz, and crossing the Carpathians, some of them had forced their way downwards (894 A. D.) to the region between the Danube and the Tisza (Parthissus). These marauders returned with the tale that

STATUE OF PRINCE ÁRPÁD

George Zala

Place of Heroes, Budapest

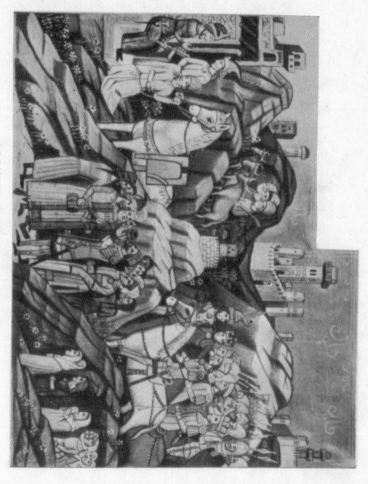

ARRIVAL OF THE HUNGARIANS

Képes Krónika XIV
Hungarian National Museum

this country was well-adapted to permanent settlement, protected as it was against invasion from the east and north by vast forests and high mountains and on the south by broad rivers. The conquest of the native population was not likely to present great difficulties. They argued in favour of the migrating Hungarians making their permanent home there, and Prince Árpád decided to take their advice and lead his followers to that land of promise.

The eastern part of the new land which was to become Hungary was, as stated above, under Bulgar rule. Indeed the Bulgars were the dominant race in the greater part of the territory between the Drave and the Save. However, after their defeat by the Hungarians, their power was so greatly impaired that they could hardly hope to defend the region north of the Danube. The prospect of the Hungarians being able to settle in those parts was therefore favourable, providing the advance were properly organized.

The soil of the coveted region was at that time held by various races. The east, — later known as Transylvania, — the district of the Tisza, and the banks of the Drave and Save were inhabited by Bulgar-Slavonic and Bulgar-Turkish races. To the east and west of Lake Balaton, Slav clans were living under the supreme rule of the Frankish Empire. The left bank of the Danube, almost as far as the river Garam was peopled by Slav races subject to the successors of the Moravian prince, Swatopluk.

It cannot be denied that the land to be occupied was but sparsely populated, but even so its inhabitants greatly outnumbered the conquering Hungarians.

It would be far from the truth to imagine that the Hungarians struck camp and set off on a migration to unknown regions, followed by a crowd of women and children and live-stock, without due preparations. Prince Árpád could not afford to risk the lives and property of his men and their families in an undertaking of which the issue was doubtful. Before they set out, the regions contemplated as their future home were reconnoitred and the mountain passes located in detail. Only then did Árpád elaborate lines of march. The Hungarians did not penetrate *en masse* and from one single direction into the country which henceforth was to be theirs. The advance took place along several routes and at intervals determined by the Prince. In this way not only were they successful in keeping the Bulgars and Petcheneggs in ignorance of their migration, but they also managed to gain a footing in different parts of the country simultaneously, thereby separating the native tribes and weakening their resistance.

Events proved that Árpád's plan was a very practical one. The breaking up of the Hungarian camps in Etelköz took place without the Bulgars or Petcheneggs being aware of what was happening. The Hungarians had long crossed the Carpathians before the news of their evacuation of Etelköz spread among the surrounding peoples. It may well be imagined what a trial of endurance it was for a people hitherto accustomed only to the plains to cross the trackless ridges of the Carpathians! What unknown dangers had to be faced in penetrating the pathless forests of the mountain-chain and forcing a way through them with their women, children and cattle, followed by carts conveying their household goods and chattels! How ardous to ford foaming torrents and wade through the marshy fens. Even a thousand years after the migration of the Hungarians the traveller from Munkács to Verecke is obliged to ford the Latorca and its tributaries forty times. And the Hungarians were forced to carry arms and occasionally to fight the inhabitants of the regions through which they passed. A marvel, indeed, that, few in number as they were, they managed to reach the Alföld (Lowlands) at all.

Today we cannot state with any accuracy their line of march, but it seems fairly certain that they approached the banks of the Tisza and Danube by different routes. A number probably entered by the passes of the South-Eastern Carpathians, or followed the course of the Lower Danube, perhaps of the Aluta or the Zsil while another body made use of the Verecke Pass, as we are told by ancient chroniclers. Be that as it may, it is undoubtedly true that as early as 898 A. D. Hungarians were in possession of the territory lying between the Drave and the Save, and had ventured as far down as the north of Italy. In the following year these Hungarians occupied the region then known as Pannonia, now Trans-Danubian Hungary, a district stretching eastward and southward of Lake Balaton. Another body of Hungarians appeared in the latter half of the year 900 in the northern parts of Trans-Danubia or Pannonia and defeating the former masters of the country, the Franks, pushed on till they reached the borders of present-day Austria. They went even farther, penetrating into Bavaria. We read that the decisive victory over the Franks was won at Bánhida. An enormous "*turul*" (a legendary eagle figuring in Hungarian heraldry) set on an eminence near the railway station at the place, commemorates the victory.

Firmly established in Pannonia, the Hungarians set about the completion of their task. The Empire of Moravia on the left bank of the Danube, though greatly depleted by the repeated onslaughts and depredations of the Bavarians, was still powerful enough to hold down a considerable part of the Hungarian forces, in case the Petcheneggs or Bulgars should attack. This probably induced Prince Árpád to make war in A. D. 902 on a Moravian Empire disintegrated by domestic troubles and party strife. He contrived to seize the territories east of the Morva and Lesser Carpathians. So the Hungarians obtained dominion over a well-watered country, particularly suitable for agriculture and cattle-breeding, and well-protected on all sides by the natural defences of the Danube, Drave, and the ring of the Carpathians.

The leader in this long struggle, the memory of which lives in Hungarian legends, was Prince Árpád. In council with the chieftains of the tribes it was he who decided the strategy to be adopted and directed the course of what fighting there was. It was he who treated with the enemy and who, when the great work of settling in the new home had been accomplished (about 902 A. D.), set about organizing public life. Tradition tells us that this was done along lines laid down by Árpád at the National Assembly held at Pusztaszer. His election as supreme ruler justified the opinion expressed by the Greek merchants that he was "a man wise in mind and in council, eminently valiant and qualified for government." When he died in A. D. 907 he was sincerely mourned by a strong, united, and well-organized nation. According to historians of a later period he was "buried with honour above the source of a little brook, the rocky bed of which runs through King Attila's city." Many believe this to have been the present Ó-Buda (Old Buda). A church was erected by a later generation on the spot where his body was laid to rest, but like many other relics of the Hungarian Middle Ages it fell into decay in course of time, and today, we can, at most merely surmise where lie the remains of Árpád, the first Hungarian Prince, to whom we owe our fatherland.

ST. STEPHEN.

997—1038.

The methods of warfare of the ancient Hungarians. Foreign raids. The camp at St. Gallen. Géza's Principality and his reconciliation with the peoples of western Europe. The spread of Christianity among the Hungarians. St. Stephen's missionary work. His coronation. Internecine warfare. St. Stephen's laws. Dispute over the Succession.

Migration through unknown and hostile territories had transformed the Hungarian tribes into a nation of rough but well-disciplined warriors. The nomadic Hungarians had always been forced to be in readiness to beat off surprise attacks. Everything was at stake. One overwhelming defeat and their wives and children would have been carried off as slaves, and their only assets, large flocks of cattle, would have passed into the enemy's hands. But in the new country they were in no such danger. On three sides, north, east, and south, they were protected by wellnigh impassable mountains, gigantic forests and broad rivers. Moreover their first encounters with their neighbours to the west had been successful enough to make them feel secure in that direction. These first conflicts with western armies brought the reassuring conviction that they were immensely superior as fighters, not only to the Moravians and Bohemians, but also to the Italians and Germans. To this feeling of superiority may be ascribed the fact that for a time the Hungarians contemplated settling permanently in Upper Italy, and continued to hold a large part of what was later to be known as Lower Austria. Even a hundred years later Vienna and its environs were a Hungarian province.

In what, one may ask, did the military superiority of the Hungarians display itself? Were they merely more numerous or more formidable in the use of weapons? We have already remarked that the number of Hungarian settlers was less than the population of Oxford and Cambridge, which proves, that numerical odds were not on their side. This military superiority, then, was solely due to their valour, endurance and method of warfare. As lightly-armed horsemen, they had the advantage of being swift and mobile. Nor were they clad in mail from head to foot like the western armies and carried no unwieldy weapons, but light slightly curved swords, and arrows that could also be used as daggers. Their bodies and horses were protected by tough but resilient leather, and they used leather shields which protected them without overtaxing man or beast, or hampering their speed in attack. Thus they were able to cover enormous distances on horseback and swoop on the enemy when least expected. Foresight and prudence characterized their tactics, not only during the period of migration through unexplored territories, but also when face to face with their foes. No attacks were made on the spur of the moment, but only when the position and strategy of the enemy had been reconnoitred. They either avoided engagements with superior forces or lured them on by feinting retreat. This was one of their favourite strategems. The main body of the army followed the line of the sham retreat until their pursuers were exhausted, and then turning on them fiercely with showers of arrows, attacked with fierce battle-cries. This usually threw the enemy into confusion and put them to flight before they could offer any serious resistance. It was a long time before the western armies became accustomed to these methods of warfare. Meanwhile they were powerless to defend themselves, and their territory lay exposed to the Hungarian raids. Greatly tempted by the prospect of easy victories and rich booty, the Hungarians continued to ravage the western countries year after year, indeed sometimes more than once a year. Fired by the irresistible urge of an adventurous spirit, the bold and hardy tribes swept through Germany, Switzerland, France and Italy, some of them venturing even as far as Spain. Though occasionally suffering a set-back, they usually returned without heavy losses. Only a bold and fearless people could have ventured on these expeditions.

The story of one of these raids has been preserved in a graphic description written by a German monk, who recorded events of which he had been the eye-witness.

In the mountainous eastern part of Switzerland, near the Austrian frontier, there stood, and still stands, a town called St. Gallen. At the time of the Hungarian conquest it was the seat of a monastery. The friars held close intercourse with the people of the neighbourhood, whom they taught various useful crafts. One day news was brought to them that the Hungarians had made their appearance in the vicinity, and would probably advance on St Gallen. The pious monks, knowing that the walls of their monastery could not withstand the onslaught of an army, prepared to make their escape. They transported the more valuable of their belongings to a neighbouring stronghold, and when the Hungarians arrived, took refuge there themselves. The Hungarians found the monastery deserted save for a single monk, who — as he himself states — could not follow his brethren, because the prior had forgotten to supply him with shoes. Heribald, as he was called, awaited the Hungarians without fear. When, to their surprise, he was discovered, they tried with the help of an interpreter to find out what he was waiting for and why he had not attempted to escape. Heribald gave the reason mentioned above. The Hungarians laughed heartily at his story and did him no harm. The friar was soon quite at home among them, and the soldiery began to question him about the valuables belonging to the monastery. Heribald was quite willing to show them the door of the treasury, which they immediately broke open. It was empty except for some candlesticks, gilded candelabras, and a few other objects not worth carrying away. Enraged and disappointed the soldiers at first threatened to flog Heribald but finally let him go and continued their search. Two

casks of wine were discovered in a cellar. Having plenty
of wine of their own, a Hungarian soldier began to
knock away the hoops of one of the casks with his battle
axe, to let the wine flow. "Spare the wine, my good
fellow" pleaded Heribald, "What are we to drink when
you are gone?" The soldier, sympathising with Heribald's anxiety, desisted and told his companions to
leave the casks alone. When sentries had been posted,
the soldiers sat down in the courtyard of the monastery
and began to make merry. Heribald took part in the
revelry, declaring afterwards that he had never partaken
of such good meats and wine. After the feast the
soldiers took to shouting and singing, and forced Heribald
and another monk who had been taken prisoner elsewhere
to sing also. Dancing, wrestling, and jousting followed,
to show the captains their prowess. But suddenly the
sound of horns announcing the approach of an enemy
interrupted their revelry. In a twinkling the soldiers
had seized their arms, and were ready to meet the foe.

This took place in 926 A. D.

It is no biassed Hungarian chronicler to whom we
owe this glimpse into the character of the Hungarian
troops. The incident was preserved from oblivion by
a German monk, and surely a German cannot be accused
of falsifying the truth, in order to present the Hungarians
in a favourable light. The record left by Heribald is
very important *evidence that the Hungarians at that period
were not the cruel savages the Germans made them out to
be, but a humane, jovial, fighting nation, fond of laughter
and song, eager to take part in contests of skill and endurance.*
A nation, moreover, united by the bonds of discipline.
Cruelty has never been a Hungarian trait. Even

AUGSBURG IN THE MIDDLE AGES

A GREAT BATTLE BETWEEN THE HUNGARIANS AND THE GERMANS
WAS FOUGHT IN THE NEIGHBOURHOOD OF AUGSBURG IN 955.

Schedel's World Chronicles (Nürnberg, 1493)

prisoners were treated with chivalry, since it was considered cowardly to torment or ill-treat defenceless foes.

As a result of these raids into foreign countries the name of our ancestors came to be dreaded by their neighbours, but in the long run the ranks of the Hungarians were being steadily reduced by these campaigns. Although few enough at first, further losses would have placed them at the mercy of a joint attack by neighbouring races. The peoples to the west, chiefly the Germans, were growing used to the military tactics of the Hungarians and were even themselves beginning to adopt them. As a result, the raiding Hungarians were so crushingly defeated on two occasions (933 A. D. and 955 A. D.) by the Germans that they ceased to raid the western countries and began to harass the Greek Empire. For some time no effective resistance was encountered, and more than once they overthrew the Greek army at the very gates of Constantinople, in full view of the inhabitants. Legend has it that one of the Hungarian chieftains, Botond by name, fought in single combat with a Greek warrior beneath the walls of the city and ran him through with his sword. But the Greeks gradually learned how to repulse these attacks, and in course of time the Hungarians were driven back.

After the death of Árpád two generations passed away in this manner. This period taught the Hungarians important lessons. Constant losses were sapping their strength, and their prestige was sinking year by year, owing to the victories of their western and southern neighbours. There was every reason to expect a united attack, for the surrounding Christian nations regarded the pagan Hungarians in their midst with the same hatred which centuries later was felt by the Christian Hungarians for the Moslem Turks when the latter conquered a great part of Hungary. It was Géza (972 to 997 A. D.), one of Árpád's successors, who first realized that the position of the Hungarians in Europe had completely changed, and that nothing short of disaster could result from the dissipation of their strength in skirmishes calculated to irritate their neighbours in the east and south. He saw the necessity of coming to terms with the adjacent peoples, and also that the reconciliation must be lasting and genuine, even if it entailed sacrifices. In order to ensure the future of his country, he went so far in his efforts to prove that the Hungarians were peaceably disposed as to welcome Christian missionaries into the land.

The German Emperor, to whose court Prince Géza despatched envoys suing for peace, received his advances gladly. It was gratifying for him to learn that the formidable race which had been a constant menace and source of irritation to Germany, was now making overtures for peace. Friendship voluntarily offered would certainly be a better guarantee of amicable relations than a peace wrested by force of arms, or gained by the wiles of diplomacy. The peace thus established between Hungary and Germany was indeed of great benefit to both countries, each monarch being henceforth free to restore and maintain order independently in his respective country. No longer was it necessary to deal with malcontents and deserters on the frontiers, who in the past had always been assured of a warm welcome and assistance on the other side. Prince Géza issued decrees strictly forbidding his people, once and for all, to make raids on other countries, and welcomed foreign missionaries to his own. These decrees were strongly opposed by the whole nation. The first to murmur were the chieftains of the tribes, who during the reign of weak princes incapable of mastering them, had become wellnigh independent rulers. Then the priets of thse pagan mysteries, who were jealous of the

PRINCE GÉZA (972—997 A. D.)
Képes Krónika XIV century
Hungarian National Museum

Christian faith in which they foresaw the decline of time-honoured rites and ceremonies and of their own power, strongly opposed Géza's innovations. The Prince himself was in a difficult position. At the bottom of his heart he was true to the ancient faith and favoured the pagan rite of sacrificing a white horse to the national god of the Hungarians. He believed in good and evil spirits,

23

in witches and gnomes, and hoped to be still a prince in the next world, where the enemies he had slain would be his henchmen. On the other hand, he was fully alive to the fact that peace between Hungary and the western nations was impossible unless he put a stop to raids and adopted Christianity. Convinced that peace and tranquility were indispensible to the Hungarians in their weakened condition, hard and ruthless measures were needed to enforce his will, cruel battles had to be fought against his own flesh and blood before he could overcome their resistance. His rule, lasting a quarter of a century, was one of constant strife and unceasing struggle against the chieftains and pagan priests. Later, in order to set an example, he embraced Christianity himself, but continued, nevertheless, to perform the ancient rites. He had his son Vajk baptized when still a child. Vajk received in baptism the name of Stephen, and was brought up in the Christian faith. By the time Prince Géza died (997 A. D.) opposition against the new order had more or less subsided. The neighbouring states were on a friendly footing with Hungary, and this was strengthened when one of Géza's daughters married the Doge of Venice and Stephen took Gizella of Bavaria to wife. The important results of Géza's policy entitle us to consider him one of our wisest and greatest princes.

When young Stephen succeeded to the heritage of his fore-fathers it seemed as if his reign was to be an untroubled one. The chieftains who had opposed his father came to render homage, and even the followers of the ancient faith were loath to make trouble for the new sovereign. Stephen was justified in hoping to be able to conclude the work initiated by his father. He had received a Christian education and was a confirmed Christian, not merely a nominal one like his father, who had accepted Christianity from motives of policy, and propagated it without believing in it. Prince Stephen was determined that his people should not be half-Christian, half-pagan. He wished to make Christianity the established state religion and to imbue every Hungarian with a firm belief therein. Well he knew the magnitude of the task, but hoped to succeed by a process of patient enlightenment. He himself set a good example. Whenever opportunity arose or necessity made it advisable, he was ready to teach, expound, and preach. By means of *viva voce* instruction he strove to induce the nation to give up its old religion and accept the new faith, of which he was an enthusiastic apostle. He had churches built and provided them with books and vestments. The Hungarian coronation robe dates from that period, and tradition says that Princess Gizella embroidered it with her own hands for the church at Veszprém, then the capital of the country. The Prince was aided in his work of converting his subjects by the Benedictine monks in Pannonhalma. This religious order built monasteries in different parts of the country, and the Benedictine friars not only devoted themselves to the propagation of the Christian faith, but also assembled the youth of the surrounding districts in their schools and taught them reading and writing. Adults received instruction in handicrafts and home industries and were taught the art of husbandry by the monks on their farms near the monasteries. Thus the monks were successful in dispelling the native distrust of the Hungarians, and Christianity soon began to spread.

25

emeric⁹

ST. STEPHEN AND HIS SON, PRINCE EMERICUS

John Thuróczy's Chronicles (Augsburg, 1488)

Every innovation has its enemies, and the new faith was no exception. It was strongly opposed by those who looked upon the decline of the old cult as a national disaster. They were not to be moved by the Prince's example and refused to listen to the teaching of the priests. Stephen therefore decided to enforce obedience by legislative measures. He made a law by which every ten villages were to have at least one church, and forbade manual work on Sunday, the Lord's Day, which was to be observed by attending Divine Service. In order to enforce his new laws he divided the country into dioceses under the jurisdiction of the Archbishop of Esztergom. The bishops were ordered to undertake the spiritual guidance of the Hungarians in their respective dioceses, to discover their needs and provide for them.

By reason of their culture and erudition they became the Prince's official advisers in matters both temporal and spiritual. But the anomalous fact remained that not only the bishops but also the parish priests and the many missionaries throughout the country were without exception foreigners. None of them spoke the Hungarian language, and being able to speak with Hungarians only through interpreters they could not bring home to them the essentials of their teachings. A change had also come over the Court of the Prince. Foreign speech and foreign customs had been introduced, partly to please the Princess, who was German, partly because the Court attracted many foreign knights and priests who were warmly welcomed by Stephen for the sake of the assistance he expected from them in his great work. But the more foreign the Court became, the more seldom did those chieftains and other Hungarians of high rank who were

27

open or secret adherents of the religion of their forebears appear in the entourage of the Prince, until at last they disappeared altogether.

Stephen himself noticed that the number of those who were abandoning the new religion and the new order and returning to the old was on the increase. He was aware that the opposition which had died down during the last years of his father's reign was reviving, and that agitation assumed menacing proportions. Determined though he was to stifle in embrio any revolutionary movement, he waited patiently in the hope of being able to avoid internecine war. Furthermore, his attention and activities were engaged in an endeavour to raise his principality to the level of the other Christian states in Europe by founding a monarchy, which besides reinforcing Hungary's international position would have made him over-lord of the chieftains. The latter continued to withhold their recognition of his suzerainty, and treated him merely as the chief of the "Magyar" tribe, which had been fortunate enough to gain ascendancy over the rest and become the greatest power in the nation. Pope Sylvester II readily complied with his request for a royal crown in recognition of his services in propagating Christianity, and Stephen had himself crowned King of Hungary at Esztergom, the capital of the country, on 15th August 1001.

The elevation of Hungary to the status of a Christian kingdom placed the country on an equal footing with other European states, conferring the same dignity and authority upon her anointed and crowned monarch as the crowned rulers of Christian Europe enjoyed. Stephen's coronation raised him above his chieftains. He styled himself "King by the Grace of God," to emphasize that fact that his royal power was independent of the will of any of his chieftains or his subjects. There remained, however, the question as to whether the enemies of the new order would acquiesce in his promotion to royalty, or attempt to restore the ancient order. The national party, with leanings towards paganism and led by Koppány, the chief of County Somogy, resolved to dethrone the King. A bitter struggle ensued between the King and Koppány, which though it ended in victory for Stephen, did not break the spirit of the opposition. Some years later the King was forced to make war on the Transylvanian army commanded by Gyula and it was only after a fierce struggle that he succeeded in strengthening the bond of union with an almost independent Transylvania and ensuring the authority of royal power there.

Having thus established peace, King Stephen took advantage of the following years to introduce great reforms. His ambition was to create a state between the Danube and the Tisza, the internal peace of which would be safeguarded by wise laws and its borders defended by a well-trained army. He it certainly was who founded the Kingdom of Hungary which to quote a national bard, "depleted but unbroken" has weathered centuries of storm and stress.

The most important of Stephen's laws in its far-reaching results was that which made it possible for private individuals to own land. Hitherto private land-owners had been unknown. The soil had been the joint property of the tribes, held in tenure by the various clans, and its cultivation was a common task. This joint ownership was abolished by Stephen. He seized the land held by the rebellious tribes and clans, and either converted it into Crown property or divided it among his loyal subjects. Indeed, he went farther and even distributed the land held by the loyal tribes, so that each of his subjects might till his own soil, as was the general custom in the western countries of Europe.

THE SACRED CROWN
OF HUNGARY

With a view to ensuring a better administration of the enormous Crown lands, he divided them into counties, over which he appointed Voivodes, responsible in time of peace for the management of the revenues and to be commanders of the troops levied in the counties in time of war. Crown revenues and the army were the two pillars upon which the might of royalty rested. The King had unrestricted command ever both and could at any time draw freely upon them for support against his enemies. His person embodied supreme authority at home and was the symbol of Hungarian unity abroad. Stephen's reign lasted four decades. In his last years the aging monarch was beset by calamities. His only son, Prince Emericus, a young man of great promise, carefully educated by St. Gerhard, Bishop of Csanád, lost his life while hunting. This aroused the question of the succession. Opinion was divided. Parties and movements sprung up, each advocating a different heir to the throne, their choice depending upon the interests of the party or clique in question, and not upon what was likely to promote the welfare of the country. That disintegration had set in even at the Court is best proved by the fact that a conspiracy was hatched to murder the old King, who escaped a violent death by mere accident. Here it may be of interest to mention that Edmund Ironside's two orphans found a home at the Court of St. Stephen. The boys had been sent to Sweden by King Canute with instructions to kill them, but the King of Sweden shrank from the thought of murdering the innocent children and despatched them to Hungary. The elder of the Princes died in his youth; the other, Edward, stayed in Hungary till 1057, when he was recalled by Edward the Confessor to succeed him on the English throne. He thereupon left Hungary accompanied by his wife Agatha, daughter of St. Stephen, and their three children, Margaret, Christina and Edgar. Later Margaret married Malcolm II of Scotland. Ethelred, Abbot of Rievaulx, who was an intimate friend of her son, David of Scotland, asserts that St. Margaret of Scotland was the descendant of "English and Hungarian kings." Edward and Agatha were followed to England

31

by a number of Hungarian nobles, who afterwards settled in Scotland. There are still some families among the Scottish nobility — e. g. the Drummonds and Leslies — which trace their descent from the Hungarian nobles in Edward's train.

King Stephen died on 15th August 1038, committing his realm to the care of the Virgin Mary, the Patroness of Hungary. Half a century after his death both he and his son Emericus were canonized. St. Stephen's day — 20th August — is observed as a national holiday, when thousands of pilgrims flock to Budapest to obtain a view of the Saint's right hand, which is carried in procession through the streets to remind people of their duty to God and the fatherland.

ST. LADISLAS.

1077—1095

Prince Béla's single combat with the captain of the Pomeranian army. Peter and Samuel Aba. Andrew I and Béla. German attack averted. St. Ladislas and Christendom. Occupation of Croatia. The Crusades. St. Ladislas performs miracles.

It was probably during the reign of Stephen that Poland, a flourishing country only recently created, was attacked by an uncivilized Slav people known as the Pomeranians. Miecislas, King of Poland, set out against them with a large army which when it came within striking distance, drew up in battle array. It was not without a certain measure of anxiety that the

King of Poland resolved to engage in a decisive battle. The forces opposing him were greatly superior to his own army, and he knew that were Poland to suffer defeat she would be laid waste. The two armies were facing each other, waiting the bugle calls to attack when suddenly the leader of the Pomeranians rode up to the Polish ranks and offered to settle the issue of the day in single combat. Instead of the troops fighting, he proposed that their leaders, or a swordsman from either side, should fight a duel in the presence of the two armies, the result of which would decide the day. The King of Poland, though surprised, found it convenient to accept the Pomeranian's offer. In spite of his advanced age and physical infirmity King Miecislas was still able to wield a sword, but he dared not risk his country's future by accepting the challenge himself and called upon his knights. Profound silence greeted his appeal, and it began to look as if the Pomeranians would win the day without striking a single blow, when an unknown knight, sword in hand, came forward and offered to take up the challenge. In the ensuing combat the unknown knight unseated the Pomeranian in full view of both armies, and the Pomeranians then did homage to the King of Poland.

The unknown knight who saved Poland from disaster was none other than the Hungarian Prince Béla. King Miecislas adopted him and gave him his daughter Richesa in marriage.

Now it may be asked how came it that Prince Béla was living incognito in Poland?

Béla and his brothers, Andrew and Levente, had been forced to flee from Hungary. King Stephen himself advised them to do so when in old age he felt too feeble and infirm to protect them against the intrigues and plots afoot in Court. In the immediate entourage of the aged King, whose days were already numbered, different parties and factions — as has been said — had arisen round the persons of the various aspirants to the throne, and these were determined to do away with any serious rivals to their favourites. As we know, one of the parties even went so far as to attempt the King's life. After this Stephen was not willing to incur the responsibility of safeguarding the lives of his nearest relatives, and urged the three surviving Princes of the House of Árpád to take refuge abroad as quickly as possible. Andrew, Béla and Levente then scattered in the surrounding countries.

The misgivings entertained by King Stephen during the last years of his life found their justification after his death. His nephew Peter succeeded him. Peter was an Italian, and he discriminated in favour of his own countrymen, appointing them to posts of honour in preference to the Hungarians. When the latter began to turn against him he sought the assistance of the Germans, preferring to sacrifice the independence of his country if he could thereby stabilize his tottering throne. The Hungarians, to whom independence was everything, were naturally enraged by this line of action. The Princes of the House of Árpád were in exile, so Samuel Aba, King Stephen's brother-in-law, rose with a considerable army against Peter and drove him from the country. Samuel Aba was elected King, but was not able to defend his throne against the Germans, with whose assistance Peter recaptured it. Instead, however, of profiting by experience and trying to appease the nation, Peter took an oath of allegiance to the German Emperor and imposed German sovereignty on Hungary. At this betrayal of the country's independence the nation again rose against King Peter and deposed him.

This took place within ten years of St Stephen's death. It was but natural that the Hungarians felt embittered upon seeing a king foreign in sentiment and spirit surrendering their country's independence to the Germans and discriminating against themselves in favour of foreigners. It was not to be wondered at if after the humiliation of seeing the Germans masters of a country from which they had hitherto been kept away, the Hungarians began to believe and proclaim that the cause of the country's downfall was the introduction of a foreign tongue and foreign customs and the denial of the ancient faith. A violent hatred of foreigners arose, and in their fury the masses turned on the strangers and Christian priests, in whom they saw the enemies of the old religion. It almost seemed as if King Stephen's work was to be undone by a national revolt. But Prince Andrew, who had been recalled from Russia, arrived in time to crush the rebellion and save the cause of Christianity. The re-establishment of internal order and peace was all the more essential since a German invasion was dreaded. It was obvious that the German Emperor, having once acquired possession of Hungary so easily, would not surrender his claim voluntarily. On the contrary, should the Hungarians resist, he was most likely to attempt the subjugation of the country. Andrew was no great fighter, and in order to protect himself against the threatened German attack he appealed to his younger and more soldierly brother, Béla, who with his wife and three sons, Géza, Ladislas and Lambert, was still living in Poland. King Andrew's envoys went to him and begged him to hasten home and defend Hungary against the pending German onslaught. King Andrew sent solemn promises to make Béla his heir, and for the time being made him independent ruler over a third part of the kingdom.

Béla, who in his heart yearned for his fatherland, accepted the proposal and returned with his family to the home of his ancestors. And in the nick of time. For the German attack followed almost immediately. Advancing with a great army towards the Hungarian frontier, they crossed it and moved forward without encountering resistance on Székesfehérvár and Esztergom. Nothing barred their way, for Prince Béla had given orders that no resistance was to be offered, and the population, who were then still living mostly in tents, were told to move with all haste to outlying districts. The enemy forces thus found a deserted country. Expecting to subsist on pillage, they were but ill-provided with food and very soon found themselves in such dire distress that the attacks of Prince Béla's horsemen in their rear ultimately broke their spirit and they finally decided to flee the country. The second German invasion in the following year also met with no success, and these two failures put an end to any further desire on the part of the Germans to tempt their luck in Hungary again.

It was hoped that after these many trials a period of peace and security would follow. A vast battlefield soaked with Hungarian blood for many years, the country was in urgent need of tranquility. But this was not to be. With the return of peace, Andrew conveniently forgot the promise he had given that on his death Béla was to inherit the crown, and took steps to secure the throne to his own son Salamon. But instead of trying to come to a peaceful agreement with his younger brother, he listened to evil advisers and conspired against Béla's life when the latter put up a fight for his rights. Once again the country was ravaged by fraternal warfare, which ended in Béla's victory, and after Andrew's death he was elected king.

His two sons had taken part at their father's side in the battles against the Germans which had insured the independence of the country. Ladislas in particular excelled both in personal valour and as a leader and it was not surprising that he became the object of the nation's wholehearted affection and admiration. Gigantic in stature, towering head and shoulders above his fellows, he was held by all to be the ideal Hungarian knight eager and willing to risk his life when the security of the country, the welfare of his Hungarian brethren, or the triumph of a just cause were at stake. Legends multiplied concerning him. Little more than a child when he returned from Poland, his very first appearance gave evidence of his personal daring. A festival was being held at Székesfehérvár in honour of Béla's and his sons' return, at which tournaments were held. Suddenly a fiery stallion, whence no one knew, charged into the ranks of the competitors, who scattered in panic. Horrorstruck they saw the stallion galloping towards Prince Ladislas, who, however, remained where he stood calmly awaiting the charge of the maddened beast, and seizing him, swung him on his back, and very soon had him completely in hand. This horse, which Ladislas named "Szög," became his favourite charger. Ladislas had taken an active part in his father's battles against the Germans. When Béla succeeded to the throne he appointed Ladislas chief captain of his forces. It was Ladislas who suppressed the second and last rising of the pagan Hungarians in the neighbourhood of Székesfehérvár and thus insured the peaceful and normal development of the country. After his revered father's death (A. D. 1063) the nation's affection and gratitude would undoubtedly have placed Ladislas on the throne, but he and his brothers declared their willingness to resign the crown in favour of Andrew's son Salamon, if the latter guaranteed them the possession of the Transylvanian regions. Salamon readily accepted this generous and unexpected offer, and the people acquiesced in an arrangement which promised order and peace. The horrors of fraternal strife were passing away but great was the danger threatening from the Petcheneggs, who at this time were living in Etelköz on the borders of Transylvania, whence they systematically began to harass Hungary through Transylvania. In A. D. 1070 great Petchenegg forces swept through the districts beyond the Tisza, and laden with booty they made hastily for the frontier to return to their own country. King Salamon and the Princes gave chase and near Cserhalom, not far from the Transylvanian frontier, they came up with the marauders. The Petcheneggs retired to the ridges of the mountain ranges, and there, drawn up in battle array, awaited the onslaught of the Hungarians up the mountain slopes. The Hungarians, overcoming every obstacle, annihilated the enemy in a fierce hand-to-hand fight, rescued the prisoners, and recaptured the booty. Prince Ladislas, pushing upwards with his troops over the mountain slopes, came upon their leader making for the frontier with a Hungarian girl in the saddle before him. Ladislas outrode the Petchenegg, killed him in single combat and rescued the girl.

The ardour of the Petcheneggs however, was not damped by this defeat and their invasion did not cease for some time to come. After the battle of Cserhalom we find them again raiding the south of Hungary. On his way home Prince Ladislas came up with them on the banks of the river Temes. Both forces were already drawn up for battle when the leader of the Petcheneggs proposed — like the Pomerians captain before him — that the issue of the day should be decided in single combat. Ladislas accepted the challenge. In the ensuing duel the leader of the Petcheneggs was slain, and the Petchenegg forces surrendered.

The Petcheneggs had been supported by the Greeks in Belgrade, called by the Hungarians Nándorfehérvár. This fort was the key to the stretches of the Lower Danube. To be master of it was to command those regions. Salamon and the Princes resolved to conquer this important strategical point. But it was well-fortified, and the siege was a prolonged one. The Greeks fought valiantly, and it almost seemed as if the attempt to take the fortress would have to be abandoned, when one stormy night a Hungarian girl, a prisoner, set the city on fire, and in the confusion the Hungarians carried the stronghold by storm. The Greek guard

39

withdrew into the *terre-plein*, but seeing the uselessness of resistance opened the gates and admitted the besieging army.

Thanks to these exploits Ladislas became exceedingly popular. But the young King Salamon, who longed to be admired and feared, began to grow jealous of his kinsman. Bards and minstrels throughout the country were singing the praises of Béla and his sons, especially Ladislas' heroic deeds, his generosity and chivalry. Legends bore the news to far-off places that Ladislas was the appointed of the Lord, the helper of the poor, of the widows and orphans, and an intrepid champion of justice. Nobody spoke about the King. His nimbus paled in comparison with that of Ladislas and his brothers. Gradually the King was possessed by envy and hate. Unscrupulous counsellers fanned the flame of these ignoble passions, until he was neither able nor anxious to hide them. From some members of the royal household the Princes learned that their lives were in danger. They decided to settle the issue by a call to arms and the bloody battle of Mogyoród ended in Salamon's defeat. The unfortunate King fled to Germany to seek the aid of his son-in-law in an attempt to regain his crown (1074).

The result of the battle of Mogyoród was hailed by all classes in Hungary as an act of Providence. To a man the whole nation embraced the Princes' cause, which was regarded as the cause of the nation itself, the more so as it was obvious that a fresh German attack was imminent. Béla's eldest son, Géza, was elected king. Under his command the German attack was broken and the independence of the kingdom saved. After a few years' reign

Géza was called to his fathers (1077) when national feeling was wholeheartedly on the side of Ladislas.

Scarcely ever has there been a king in history upon whose reign such wide-spread hopes were set as upon that of Ladislas. And perhaps there has never been another Hungarian king whose rule — a comparatively short one of 21 years (1077—1095) — left such monuments behind it as his. Civil wars and the campaigns against Germany had not failed to leave their mark upon the national spirit. After all, even the exiled Salamon had some personal followers, who though outwardly loyal to Géza and Ladislas, would have been ready at any moment to support an attempt to depose the brothers. Then again the German attacks had agitated afresh those of the population who regarded the Christian faith as the root of every evil that had befallen the nation in that it favoured and facilitated foreign influence. This party was convinced that a return to the faith of their forebears was the only effective safeguard of national independence. King Ladislas did not fail to consider these elements, which at any moment might disturb the peace of his reign. He was anxious to solve these difficulties once and for all. This explains the fact that from the moment of his accession he tried to come to an agreement with the unfortunate Salamon, who indeed accepted his proposals. The agreement arrived at did not restore the crown to Salamon, but assured him an eminent, privileged position in public life. By this move, which proved that his aims were just and his intentions peaceful and free from any mental reservations, Ladislas won over those still loyal to Salamon. When that unstable spirit again began to intrigue against the King the latter's newly gained partisans refused to

41

support him in his plot to murder Ladislas. The King was obliged to imprison Salamon and not a single word was raised in his favour, for all were convinced that right and justice were on the King's side. It was a far more difficult task *to persuade those attached to the ancient faith that they were mistaken in assuming that the Christian religion was the chief source of all the trials and humiliations that had overtaken the country*. The lessons of the two previous pagan risings, so cruelly crushed, made Ladislas see clearly the impossibility of changing the creed of the nation by political measures, or even by force of arms. His conviction grew that no permanent results were to be expected in this province except by way of conversion and with the aid of an inspiring personal example. He determined to supply that example himself, and to prove by deeds as well as words that to be both a Christian and a Hungarian was not a contradiction in terms, and that a man might be a faithful Christian without having to sacrifice his national feelings. When in the first years of his reign a bitter conflict arose between the Pope and the German Emperor over questions of political power, he sided with neither in order to be free to cast his vote as his heart dictated. When called upon to give his decision, he never lost sight of the interests of his own people even when this sometimes meant taking sides against the Pope and sometimes against the German Emperor. That Christianity ultimately became the national religion in Hungary was his work. It was thanks to the personal example set by the King that it became more and more firmly rooted in the country. When towards the end of his reign he published a new code of laws to meet changed conditions, it was no longer necessary to impose severe punishments on those who still clung to the old faith. Paganism was gradually and imperceptibly vanishing. How advanced Christian civilization in Hungary was in the days of Ladislas may be judged from the fact amongst others that the Anglo-Saxons who after the Battle of Hastings (1066) followed the Earl of Gloucester to Constantinople and from thence — probably years later — to the shores of the Black Sea, where they settled in a region which they named New England, sent to Hungary for bishops and priests to preserve them in the Faith.

Owing to his strict but equitable laws, internal peace and order were being slowly restored. This meant a great increase in strength. It made defence an easier task, and later paved the way to more ambitious ventures. The expeditions undertaken by the King, sometimes in very difficult circumstances, against the Petcheneggs, the Cumanians and the Russians, safeguarded the territorial integrity of the country and spread the fame of Hungarian arms throughout Europe. The occupation of Croatia and its union with the Hungarian Kingdom in 1091 testified to the fact that a nation conscious of its own power and ready to exert it had become firmly established in the territories encircled by the Carpathians. Since the day the Hungarians had settled in those regions the occupation of Croatia was the first territorial expansion, and for a long period subsequently it indicated the course Hungarian foreign policy was to pursue.

At this time Hungary was a country where peace and order prevailed — a land inhabited by a law-abiding, single-minded people governed by a just monarch. The attention of the Christian nations of Europe was directed

43

to King Ladislas and his country, and when a leader was sought for the Crusades, his name became prominent. The Europe of that day was all afire to deliver the Holy Land from the Turk. Armed hosts were awaiting an inspired chief to lead them in a campaign under the sign of the Cross against the infidels. General opinion declared in favour of the King of Hungary, tales of whose valour, strategic skill and sincere Christianity were told in the western countries, and whose leadership would have been accepted by all. But his sudden death on 29th July 1095 prevented one of the greatest expeditions ever recorded in the history of the European nations from setting out under a Hungarian flag.

Within a hundred years of his death the Church canonized King Ladislas. Even during his lifetime many tales and legends were in circulation about him. It was said, for instance, that with God's help he drew water from a rock to quench the thirst of his troops. That in answer to his prayer on behalf of his hungry army, a herd of stags appeared, and instead of taking flight at the sight of the soldiers, came tamely into the camp. Once when he had routed the Cumanians somewhere in Transylvania, the enemy, in order to save their lives, scattered their looted gold and jewels on the road, hoping cupidity would tempt their pursuers to stop and pick up the treasure and thereby give them time to escape. But the King prayed to God and lo! the gold and jewels were turned into pebbles. About 1093 the black plague was raging in Hungary. Ladislas, at war in Russia, was informed of this peril at the moment of returning home. He began to pray, and in a dream an angel appeared to him and bade him shoot an arrow into the air and search for the spot where it fell.

STATUE OF ST. STEPHEN, KING OF HUNGARY

Aloysius Strobl

Fishers' Bastion, Budapest

ST. LADISLAS' RELIQUARY

XIV century
Győr, Cathedral

He did so, and found an herb the juice of which was a cure for the plague, which soon afterwards ceased.

In Transylvania, of which he afterwards became the patron saint, Cserhalom, the Gorge of Torda and other innumerable spots are sacred to the memory of his miraculous deeds. Nagyvárad, a bishopric founded by Ladislas, has always been a place of pilgrimage for Hungarians. Some centuries later King Louis the Great went there on a pilgrimage, and kneeling on St. Ladislas' tomb, vowed that he would endeavour to be a king worthy of his great ancestor. The last legend connected with St. Ladislas dates from the time of this same Louis the Great. In 1345 the Tartars descended on Transylvania. Their invasion was checked by the Siculians, who after three day's fighting, succeeded in throwing them back. Legend says that on these days St. Ladislas' body disappeared from the church in Nagyvárad, and when found later in its usual place, to everybody's amazement the corpse was covered with sweat like the body of a man who had been doing hard work. An old Tartar was heard to declare that he had seen St. Ladislas fighting in the ranks among his beloved Siculian people, and that it was his presence that turned the tide of battle. Modern poets, as well as medieval chroniclers have found inspiration in the legends and tales surrounding the figure of St. Ladislas. The works of John *Garay (Garay János)*, Michael *Vörösmarty (Vörösmarty Mihály)*, John *Arany (Arany János)*, Michael *Tompa (Tompa Mihály)* and others show that the reign of St. Ladislas was the most splendid period in the age of Hungarian chivalry. Each tale in the annals of that era has preserved records of Hungarian valour and fame for posterity.

KING COLOMAN.

1095—1116

*Coloman and Álmos.   The crusades.   The conquest of Dal-
matia.   The laws of King Coloman.   Belief in witches.
Trial of witches.*

Ladislas had no male issue.   His only daughter,
Piroska, married the heir to the Byzantine throne.   The
crown of St. Stephen would consequently descend to one
of his brother Géza's sons — either Coloman or Álmos.
King Ladislas regarded them as the presumptive heirs to
the throne.   His own reign having been one of incessant
struggle against enemies endeavouring to overthrow his
kingdom, the qualities he most desired in his successor
were courage and valour.   For a long time therefore he
preferred to think of his younger nephew Álmos, as his
immediate successor.   Álmos was a fighter.   He gladly
took part in the different campaigns and in soldiering
found the zest of life.   Later, however, the King noticed
certain deficiencies in his character, and turned his attention to the elder of the two brothers, Coloman or *Kálmán*,
who though not lacking in courage, preferred books and
learning to the stress of war.   This trait earned for him
the nick-name of "*Könyves Kálmán*" (Bookish Coloman).
Coloman was one of the most outstanding figures among
the kings of Hungary in the Middle Ages.   His wise
laws, far-seeing foreign policy and successful defence of
the country's territorial integrity make his name memor-
able in the history of Hungary.   At the time of his accession to the throne all Europe was humming with preparations for a crusade to liberate the Holy Land.   Men

46

flocked to fight under the banner of the Cross, and set out for the East in small and large bodies led by adventurous knights. In many cases no adequate preparations had been made for the campaign, and in order to subsist the crusaders were often guilty of acts of violence in the countries through which they passed. Terrifying rumours were in circulation all over Europe. This decided King Coloman to refuse the crusaders passage through Hungary, and he met them with an army at the frontier. The crusaders, unwilling to change their route, resorted to arms, and the King had a hard struggle to disperse these vagrant bands. But the main body of the crusaders was well disciplined and King Coloman not only allowed it to cross the frontier, but also provided plentifully for its needs (1096). After the march of the crusaders King Coloman was chiefly preoccupied for many years with events in Croatia. Authority in Croatia was invested in Prince Álmos, who received the title of King when Ladislas entrusted him with the administration of this newly acquired province. But Álmos did not know how to manage the Croatians, who in 1097 rose in open revolt against him. After a thorough investigation of local conditions, King Coloman felt obliged to recall his brother. This decision and other just measures finally restored peace. His dealings with the Croatians further matured in his mind the idea of acquiring possession of the Dalmatian sea-board. On the one hand he felt that a Hungary with a free outlet to the sea would be a greater power in Europe, and on the other he was convinced that the relations between Hungary and Croatia would be much stronger if the sea-board to the west of the latter also acknowledged Hungarian supremacy. This plan he carried out. He conquered Dalmatia and all its rich towns surrendered to him. But this new conquest aroused the hostility of the Venetian Republic. The latter was dependent on the Dalmatian forests for timber, and furthermore the establishment of the Hungarians on the coast was a menace to the naval supremacy and commercial interests of Venice. From this time on bitter warfare was waged between Venice and Hungary for the possession of Dalmatia. But apart from adding to the prestige of Hungary as a military power it profited her nothing.

It was not alone in the sphere of foreign policy that King Coloman followed in the footsteps of his great predecessor, but also in his domestic administration. He made every effort to consolidate internal conditions, one of the most important tasks undertaken by the saintly King Ladislas. He framed laws adapting civil and ecclesiastical administration, and taxation to the requirements of the age. On the whole his laws were more lenient than those of St. Ladislas, which, for instance, punished theft with death, and in which ordeals by fire, etc. still played a prominent part. King Coloman made the testimony of witnesses the basis of all evidence. This was a step towards modern ideas, as were the measures which punished murder with greater severity than offences against property. The most momentous of his reforms, however, was the banning of witches' trials. King Coloman forbade them on the grounds that "witches do not exist."

In the Middle Ages people believed in two kinds of witches. The one, the *striga*, was supposed to be a nocturnal, blood-sucking vampire. The rest, sorceresses, were credited with being able with the devil's aid to

bring every misfortune on mankind, from blasting their
cattle and making the cows run dry to inflicting diseases
upon people and even causing death by philtres, en-
chantment, and other secret rites.   King Coloman's law
applied to the *strigae*, but not to the sorceresses in whom

KING COLOMAN
John Thuróczy's Chronicles (Augsburg, 1488)

he still firmly believed, as all men did at that time and
for centuries later.   The belief in sorceresses led to the
trials for witchcraft which were so frequent in Europe,
chiefly in France, Germany and Italy,   and which
brought death in a most cruel form on thousands.   These
trials were not unknown in Hungary either, and it was
only in 1768 that Maria Theresa abolished them for good.

As far as we can judge 169 persons were burnt at the stake for witchcraft in Hungary between 1565 and 1756, a period of nearly two centuries. The number is appalling enough, but nothing compared with the figures for the western countries of Europe. In 1589, for instance, on one single day 133 persons were burnt at Quedlinburg in Germany. At another place 360 persons suffered the same death in seven years (from 1587 to 1593), and a French Judge openly admitted having sent *several thousand* sorceresses to the stake.

Hungary could not remain untainted by the influence of ideas prevailing throughout Europe. But in Hungary the persecution of witches never assumed such proportions as in western Europe. Certain it is that King Coloman's denial of the existence of at least one kind of witch proved him far in advance of his age. If to this we add the other achievements of his reign (1095—1116) we are fully justified in including him among our greatest rulers.

KING BÉLA III.

1173—1196

Discovery of Béla III's tomb in Székesfehérvár. Hungary and the Byzantine Empire. Béla at the Greek Court. Difficulties attending his accession to the throne of Hungary. The Royal Chancellorship. Hungary and France. The Cistercians. Economic evolution. The crusades.

At Székesfehérvár in the year 1848 the drains close to the wall surrounding the Episcopal Residence were being mended. On December 5th workmen uncovered some marble slabs, and when these were removed several marble coffins came to light. One of them contained a skeleton and some jewels. Excavations were undertaken by archæologists, and it was found that the Episcopal Residence and Gardens covered the site of the cathedral erected by St. Stephen and destroyed in 1601 by the Turks. It was known that this church had been the burying place of the Kings of Hungary, and it seemed probable that the marble coffins contained the remains of some of them and possibly of their wives. Further excavations revealed that the workmen had stumbled on the ashes of one of the greatest kings of the Árpádian dynasty, Béla III (1173—1196), and those of his first wife, Queen Anne, who died in 1184. Pure accident led to this discovery, for none of the tombs of the thirty-five kings of Hungary reigning between St. Stephen and the battle of Mohács (1526) have been discovered by posterity except this one. The rest of the Royal tombs were destroyed by the ravages of war. Now the ashes of Béla III and his Queen rest in the Church of the Virgin in Buda, where they were reverently deposited by the nation in 1897.

During the youth of Béla III Hungary was at war with the Byzantine Empire, which was then awakening to new strength. The Greek Emperor Emmanuel was a son of St. Ladislas' daughter, Piroska. His ambition was to create a mighty empire including Hungary. King Coloman's successors (Stephen II, 1116—1131; Béla II or Béla the Blind, 1131—1141; Géza II, 1141—1161) were weaklings. Internecine wars for the crown had depleted the country's vitality and campaigns waged on foreign countries on the feeblest of pretexts had lowered its prestige. Enfeebled and torn, Hungary was not likely to be able to hold her own against so powerful a sovereign as Emmanuel. The Emperor made serious preparations to invade Hungary with a great army, and for many years skirmishes were the order of the day on the southern frontier. Sometimes the Hungarians were the victors, sometimes the Greeks. There was a period when Emmanuel's slightest wish was law in Hungary and he was able to set up rival kings to Stephen III (1161—1172) who had been legitimately crowned. Emmanuel did this assuming that his nominees would be willing tools in his hands. Later, however, the Hungarian army repulsed the Greek invaders and forced the Emperor to sue for peace. Much blood was shed on both sides, but Hungary successfully defended her frontiers and checked Emmanuel's aggressive designs. Hungary's stubborn resistance brought the Emperor to a peculiar decision. Realizing that he could never bring about Hungary's union with the Greek Empire by force of arms, he conceived the idea of doing so by means of family ties. In 1163 he invited Stephen III's younger brother, Béla, to the Imperial Court and promised to betroth him to his daughter and make him his successor. He evidently held that a Prince of the House of Árpád wearing the Greek Imperial crown would command such respect among Hungarians that on the throne becoming vacant he would be elected King of Hungary. For several years therefore Béla was treated by the Imperial Court as the heir apparent to the Hungarian crown, and in accordance with the Emperor's wishes all the powerful within the Empire pledged their faith to him. When, however,

52

Emmanuel's second wife bore him a son, his fatherly instincts began to assert themselves. The Emperor was still obsessed with the dream of a world-wide empire, but he relinquished the idea of seeing the two crowns united on Béla's head. Thus it came that he had his newborn son crowned Emperor, and also broke off his daughter's engagement to Béla, in order to preclude the possibility of the Hungarian Prince eventually aspiring to the Imperial crown which henceforth the Emperor naturally desired to secure to his own son. It was with something like relief, therefore, that Emmanuel received the news of the death of Stephen III and learned that the crown of Hungary had been offered to and accepted by Béla.

The years spent at the Imperial Court did not fail to leave their impression on Béla. It was a world foreign to him, one which at first he did not understand, and in which — so different was it in character from everything Hungarian — he never really felt at home. Nevertheless he was compelled to see that the Greek Empire was well-organized. Administration, finances, the army and diplomacy were a smoothly running machine, the control of which was in the hands of the Emperor. Internal and foreign policy were united and harmonious. The circumstances were in many respects totally different from those in Hungary. The constitution of the Greek Empire, its past history, its religion and its civilization were utterly different, as were all its political aspirations. But it was not to be denied that this foreign world was rich in customs and institutions the introduction and assimilation of which seemed imperative for Hungary, if she was not to be left behind

53

by the great and progressive European nations. On the way home the mind of the Hungarian Prince was occupied with thoughts of reform. He crossed the frontier with the determination to establish in Hungary all the institutions which had proved a success in the Byzantine Empire, and for lack of which, in his opinion, Hungary could not enter upon the path of progress and development.

But at home a great disappointment awaited him. He was not received with that unanimous affection which he desired and the absence of which he had felt so keenly in the entourage of the Emperor.

In the first place his own mother felt coldly towards him, and made no effort to conceal the fact that a son who had passed so many years abroad seemed almost a stranger, and that she would have preferred to see the crown rest on his younger brother, Géza, whom she herself had educated. Béla was also regarded with suspicion by the Church, at the head of which was the austere Archbishop of Esztergom. The cause of this mistrust was a current rumour that Béla and his wife, Anne of Antioch, Emmanuel's sister-in-law and French by birth, had been converted to the Oriental Orthodox faith. A large section of the nation also awaited Béla without enthusiasm because he came accompanied by Greek forces, and nobody knew whether there was not some pact detrimental to Hungary between him and the Emperor. It was a long time before Béla was able to consider himself master of the situation, and even then mastery had to be purchased at a great price. He broke off relations with his mother, whom he banished to Greece where she spent the rest of her stormy life in a nunnery. He imprisoned his younger brother, Géza, who did not regain his liberty until twelve years had passed. It was no easy matter either to dispel the distrust of the Church. The priests were jealous for the interests of the Catholic religion which Béla, they suspected, had most likely forgotten at the Greek Court or denied at the Emperor's request when he still hoped for the Imperial crown. They therefore refused to support him until he had furnished further evidence of being a true son of the Catholic Church.

It must be admitted that Béla was always ready to oblige Emmanuel, even to the extent of sending armed assistance in times of need, but he never allowed the Greek Emperor to interfere in the affairs of Hungary, the independence of which he considered his first duty to safeguard. On Emmanuel's death (1180) he hastened to re-incorporate Sirmium and Dalmatia in the Hungarian Kingdom. These provinces had been wrested from Hungary by Emmanuel, and their restoration again opened up the way to the sea.

At first Béla contented himself with the task of re-establishing order and authority, but he never lost sight of the reforms on which his heart was set. One of his most important acts was to institute an office called the Royal Chancellory, the function of which was to preserve a record of every matter that came before the King, so that the royal decrees and judgments should not pass into oblivion. Every person who received estates from the Crown or otherwise, and every litigant whose lawsuit had been decided, received a written deed or document of sorts from the Chancellory which enabled him and his heirs to prove and defend their rights. The Royal Chancellory had therefore an important influence on the evolution of civil law and civil rights. Furthermore, it was instrumental in spreading a knowledge of reading and writing; a deed or document being of little value to its owner unless he could read and understand it. The post of an official in the Royal Chancellory — notaries, they were called — was no sinecure. Manifold and diverse were the matters dealt with, and frequently extremely involved. Only experts in legal and judicial affairs — men who were no mean scholars either — could attain that office by royal appointment. One of them was the notary who was known by the Latin appellation of *Anonymus*, and was the first to write a description of the origin, migrations, settlement and foreign raids of the Hungarians. His monument by Nicolas Ligeti — portraying the scholar lost in thought — adorns the City Park in Budapest.

Béla III was particularly anxious to spread civilization in his country. His conviction was that only a civilized nation could be rich and independent. France was the ideal he desired to imitate. He was also bound to her through family ties after 1186, when he took to wife the sister of Philip Augustus II, King of France. Thanks to this, during his reign and for some years later many hundreds of young Hungarians went to study at the University of Paris which at that time was the centre of European learning. Graduates returning to their own respective countries became the propagators and teachers of advanced western culture. An even more immediate influence on civilization in Hungary was exerted by the Cistercian monks who were brought from France by the King. It is well-known that this Order has always devoted itself with praiseworthy results to teaching and preaching. In Béla's days they were chiefly occupied with agriculture, and thereby won the confidence of a race engaged almost exclusively in the art of husbandry. The friars, even those among them who were scions of the highest aristocratic families, put their hands to the plough, the spade, and the hoe to show their respect for labour and labourers and to teach the nobles and knights to honour the common people and their tasks. They were warmly welcomed everywhere and soon won the confidence of those among whom they settled. At that time the soil of the country was for the most part a barren waste waiting to be developed for farming, and the people had to learn how to reclaim the swamps and fell primeval forests. The Cistercians did not erect their monasteries in open fertile districts designed by Nature for agriculture, but — in order to develop the virtues of discipline and strengthen the character of the monks — in rough, wooded or marshy regions. The diligent monks had to fight Nature at every step, and it was only by dint of the hardest toil that they could transform the wastes into arable land and grazing pastures. The fame of their model farms reached people in the remotest districts, who came to learn the art of profitable husbandry, which not only added to their own welfare, but also promoted the economic development of the country.

Evolution in farming naturally led to prosperity in other branches of economy. Within the precincts of the monasteries and in the Sepusian and Transylvanian regions, where the Saxons had settled down during the reign of Béla's father, Géza II, a remarkable industrial and commercial growth set in, which in the course of time began to attract the attention of other countries. By then the western peoples had acquired some knowledge of Hungary and her inhabitants, especially at the time of the crusades, when the Valley of the Danube was the route for armies on the march to the East. Later Hungary became a link in the chain of international trade, the highways of which led through her territory to the great markets of the East and West. Numerous foreigners began to settle in the cities, — chiefly French, Italian and German tradesmen. They introduced new handicrafts and opened up foreign markets for raw materials. Thanks to the policy inaugurated by Béla III Hungary was on the way to become the most important agricultural country of Central Europe.

The centre of the life of the country was the Royal Court. Adopting the Greek Imperial Court as his model, Béla ruled in magnificent splendour. He could afford to do so with an income in gold that enable him to vie with the richest European sovereigns. His Court, above all after his second marriage, attracted many foreigners, chiefly French, many of whom settled in Hungary and became the ancestors of numerous noble families. To the Royal Court was brought news and knowledge from the remotest parts not only of the Kingdom of Hungary, but of the whole known world. Speedy and reliable information was always to be obtained there about everything that concerned Hungary and rest of the civilized world. The King was greatly interested in the events in the Holy Land. The Royal Court was astounded to learn that the Sultan of Egypt had annihilated the crusaders and taken Jerusalem. It was Béla's brother-in-law, the King of France, who first informed the King that he had taken up the championship the Cross, and that following his example, the King of England and the German Emperor had likewise decided to recover the Holy Land from the infidels. Their expedition (1189) failed however, and they were unable to retake Jerusalem. But the nations of Europe were not disheartened. On the contrary, it stimulated them to constantly renewed efforts. Then it was that King Béla decided (perhaps encouraged by the Queen who was a zealous supporter of the crusades) to join the next expedition. But while making ready he fell ill, and feeling that he would not recover, he charged his younger son Andrew to go to the Holy Land and in his place fulfil his vow under pain of a father's curse. Béla died on 23rd April, 1196, comforted by the knowledge that he had raised his kingdom from ignominy and isolation to a wealthy, a powerful state that made its ruler the equal of the German Emperor, the head of Western Christianity.

KING BÉLA IV.

1235—1270

Julian the Monk's pilgrimage to the ancestral country. News of the Tartar menace. Hungary under the decendants of Béla III. Andrew II and the Golden Bull. Accession of Béla IV. The advent of the Cumanians. Defensive measures against the Tartars. The battle of Muhi and its consequences. Ruin. Recovery. Béla IV and Stephen V.

The Hungarians had now been living some centuries in the basin of the Carpathians, but the tales of their first home never faded in the thoughts of the succeeding generations. Merchants and pilgrims told of Magyars living somewhere in the far East who were masters of a great independent country. No exact information, however, was forthcoming, but what was known was enough to fire the imagination of the Magyars in Hungary. Finally, about the year 1235 two Dominican friars, Julian and Bernard, decided to find the ancient home of the nation and bring back authentic news instead of tales and legend, and, if possible, establish direct communication between the two bodies of Magyars, or as they are called in English, Hungarians.

Their journey was beset by hardships. Brother Bernard died of privation on the way. But Julian continued with unflagging zeal towards the East, following up all the clues he found on his way. His perseverance was eventually rewarded, for he found the ancient land of the Hungarians where he was received with the greatest kindness. The inhabitants were able to understand his speech and listened with sympathetic ears when he told of the dangers and hardships endured by their kin who had migrated westward centuries earlier, but whose memory still lived dimly in the old country. He was happy to be able to verify the reports of a far-off ancestral home and was proud to be the first to obtain authentic information about his people's brave and wealthy kinsmen in the Far East. He lived to arrive safely in the Valley of the Danube, and report all he had seen and heard. It was from him that our ancestors first learned with certainty that "Old Hungary" was no myth or traveller's tale but a reality, and that Hungarians there were eager to renew those ties connecting them with Hungarians in the west. But Julian's tale was not all pleasant hearing. He also told of an approaching peril which threatened the inhabitants of the old country filling them with anxiety for the future. Some years earlier the Mongols, or Tartars as they were then called, had founded a mighty empire in Asia somewhere to the east of ancient Hungary. It was said that the Mongols intended to subjugate not only Asia, but also Europe, in which case both the ancestral country of the Hungarians and the western Hungarian Kingdom would be endangered. News of Julian's travels and his

KING ANDREW II (1205—1235)
John Thuróczy's Chronicles (Augsburg, 1488)

discovery were brought to Béla IV, who was eager to hear about his Hungarian kindred in the east, but the possibility of a Tartar invasion filled him with anxiety and alarm. Hungary was at this time no longer so strong and powerful as she had been but half a century earlier in the reign of

61

Béla III. Under the rule of Béla IV's immediate predecessors, Emery (1196—1204) and Andrew II. (1205—1235), fraternal strife had again sapped the strength of the country and greatly increased the power of the oligarchs, who on various pretexts had seized large numbers of the royal estates and were oppressing the lesser gentry and serfs. Decline was especially noticeable under Andrew II. This monarch had proved a thoughtless master who improvidently dissipated his sources of revenue and the royal estates, and was even known to bestow a whole country on a single favourite. He spent his revenues as lavishly as though his resources were inexhaustable. Counterfeit money was in circulation throughout the country, which paralysed trade and commerce. Taxes were continually raised and exacted without mercy from the indignant population by collectors who were mostly of another race. The poor were without protection. The laws were excellent but nobody enforced them, and to crown all, King Andrew, in order to please his German wife, discriminated in favour of his German subjects. This led to a conspiracy one of the victims of which was the Queen herself. This event is the subject of Joseph Katona's masterpiece "*Bánk Bán.*" Hungary's decay was a source of great anxiety to the King's elder son, the noble Prince Béla, as well as to all right-minded Hungarians. They saw clearly that unless the system in force underwent a fundamental change, the country would be ruined and become an easy prey to her neighbours. Dreading what the future might hold, they at first tried to persuade the King to abandon the course he was pursuing, but seeing the impossibility of influencing him, they convoked a meeting of the Estates of the Realm and forced the King to acknowledge the laws of the land. These laws were then collected and embodied in a codex, and the King was made to swear an oath that he would respect them (1222). This document was called the Golden Bull, because it had a golden seal attached to it. It consisted of thirty-one points, in which the duties of the monarch and the nobility (which did not mean the aristocracy alone, but all who were not serfs) were clearly set forth. The intention was to obviate the possibility of any conflict arising in future between the monarch and the nation. The Golden Bull has ever since been the basis of the Hungarian Constitution. With the lapse of time some of its points have been modified, but in essentials its validity has been preserved throughout the centuries, and it has continued to be the pattern upon which Hungarian public life has been moulded. Here let it be said in passing that the Golden Bull of Hungary (1222) followed closely on the heels of the English Magna Charta (1215), and that they both were the foundations of the respective Constitutions. The surprising similarity in form and substance between the Golden Bull and the Magna Charta (the *jus resistendi*, for instance, is the last point in both) seems to prove that the drafters of the Golden Bull had a knowledge of the Magna Charta. Indeed, we have records showing that the Primate of Hungary was the guest of Stephen Langton, the drafter of the Magna Charta, at Canterbury in 1220, *i. e.* two years before the Golden Bull was issued. We also know that Thomas, Bishop of Eger, spent several months with some of the Barons of the Magna Charta during the siege of Danietta, a port of Egypt, and that Robert — one of the most eminent of the Hungarian bishops — was of English origin.

Had Andrew II strictly adhered to the Golden Bull, internal peace and normal evolution would have been assured for a considerable length of time. But the weak King, lending his ear to evil counsel, continued

ST. ELIZABETH, DAUGHTER OF ANDREW II

to manage the affairs of the country as though no such document existed, and national decline continued its downward course. In vain did Prince Béla more than once intercede. Even the energetic protests of the Primate of Hungary, the Archbishop of Esztergom, were as the "voice of one crying in the wilderness."

64

Andrew could not or would not change his conduct and things went on as before until 1235 when he died.

Upon his father's death Béla IV ascended the throne of a decaying, divided, and impoverished country. He was guided by ripe and sound judgment. He knew the history of the difficult years and was well-aware what the causes of the dissension had been. He inaugurated energetic reforms and after several years of untiring work succeeded, though at the cost of making many enemies, in laying the foundations of untroubled development and in re-establishing the prestige of the country in the eyes of Europe. Peace alone was needed to insure permanent progress. It was therefore with the greatest concern that the King listened to the monk Julian's tale of an imminent Mongol attack. The whole future of the Country depended upon the truth or falsehood of the report, for it was questionable whether a Hungary but so recently recovered would be able to repel an invasion. The reports of the Mongol advance — alas! — proved only too true. Resistance was of no avail. The old home of the Hungarians had fallen along with all the greater and lesser countries situated in the territory now known as Siberia and Russia. In 1239 a piteous delegation appeared at Béla's Court from the Cumanian king, Kötöny. These bearers of woeful tidings reported the conquest by the Tartars of the powerful Cumanian Empire. King Kötöny himself had only escaped being carried off into slavery by fleeing with his people, to the number of about forty thousand families, to the regions of the Lower Danube. King Kötöny now feared that even that place of refuge would not afford a secure asylum for his followers, and he asked permission to settle down in Hungary, promising to help to defend the country against the common foe.

King Béla pondered earnestly on the situation. The advent of the Cumanians would mean considerable reinforcement, and convinced that the Tartars were at his gates, it would have seemed folly on his part to reject the proffered help. He therefore eagerly assented and settled the Cumanians in the valleys of the Danube and Tisza, where the names Great and Little Cumania have surrired to this day. But the settlement of the Cumanians gave rise to unforeseen difficulties. They were heathen, and like other nomadic folk, unruly, and they could not be made to understand that they must confine themselves to the territory allotted to them. They constantly harrassed the Hungarian population and did not even refrain from acts of violence. Thus the sympathy of the Hungarians was soon lost to them. Complaints were lodged against them almost daily at the Royal Court. The population sued for protection and applied to the King or the Viceroy (the Palatine) for redress of their grievances. Béla was in a difficult predicament. On the one hand it could not be questioned that the complaints against the Cumanians were justified, but on the other to coerce them might result in Kötöny and his followers turning their backs on the Hungarians and leaving Hungary in the lurch at the moment when help was most needed. Influenced by this consideration the King showed marked leniency towards the Cumanians, and very often settled controversies by discriminating in their favour which enraged the Hungarians. In any case many of the latter were bitter against the King for the manner in which he had relentlessly swept away unjustice and oppression and restored order throughout the country. Public opinion worked itself to such a pitch of excitement and exasperation against the Cumanians that the King thought it wise to bring Kötöny and his family to the Royal Court, where they would be under his personal protection. Then he distributed the Cumanians in larger or smaller colonies in different parts of the kingdom, hoping they would adopt the customs and laws of the land and abandon their acts of violence. But the Cumanians refused to adapt themselves to their new surroundings, and complaints poured in from every part of the country to the Royal Court in an increasingly menacing manner, demanding strong measures against them. The King, who was in possession of reliable information concerning the impending onslaught of the Mongols, was less than ever inclined to treat the Cumanians with a high hand. His reluctance to do so soon led to his isolation till at last he found himself opposed by the entire country.

By the winter of 1240—41 it was obvious that the enemy might be expected to strike in a few months. The King did not pass the winter months in idleness. Announcing to all concerned that the Tartars were planning the conquest not only of Hungary, but also of Europe, and that the fate of the latter would be decided in Hungary, he solicited urgent aid from the Pope, the German Emperor, and the neighbouring monarchs. Meanwhile he blockaded the passes of the Carpathians, and sent troops to defend the frontier. At home he called every able-bodied man to arms. To symbolize the magnitude of the danger and to impress it upon all, he ordered blood-stained swords to be carried through every county.

His appeal for help was doomed to disappointment. A bitter struggle was being waged between Pope and Emperor, and neither of them would send assistance to the King. Of all concerned, only Frederick, Duke of Austria, was inclined to support him, but the body of men which he led personally to the walls of the city of Pest was scarcely more numerous than his usual hunting train. In Hungary itself the people regarded the blood-stained swords with indifference. Some there were who even refused to credit the report that the Tartars were coming. Others said that if the King was going to war, he should do so with his favourite Cumanians. But all were alarmed when the news came that the Mongols had crossed the Carpathians without difficulty, and having crushed the lines of defence, were pouring into the country. Now at length people hastened to take up arms. They hurried to the King's camp. But only a few of them reached it, for the Tartar hordes, sweeping down like a whirlwind, wiped out the greater part of them on their march.

The Tartars followed a preconceived plan of campaign. Regarding Hungary as the strongest country in Central Europe, where the chance of their establishing a footing in Europe would be decided, their plan of attack was to isolate her from all foreign help and prevent the Hungarians from rallying round the King in their customary manner. Acting on this plan, Batu Khan the leader of the Tartars, sent a great army into Poland. It crushed the Polish forces and invaded Hungary from the north-west along the river Vág. The main body

68

of the Tartar army under Batu Khan's leadership entered the country through the pass of Verecke, while greater or smaller contingents made their way through the Transylvanian passes, advancing towards the great Hungarian plain (the Alföld), the object of which was to annihilate the various Hungarian units before they could concentrate.

By the end of March 1241 the agile Tartar horsemen were already encircling the walls of Pest, and in spite of the rallying Hungarians, they burned the surrounding village and granaries, after storming every town and village on the way. The Hungarians encamped in Pest were greatly enraged to see the sky red with the flames of surrounding villages, but were unable to seek vengeance, for the King, in order to conserve his strength, had forbidden sallies and sporadic attacks, though the Royal veto was not binding on the Duke of Austria. Frederick, to show his bravery, repeatedly hurled himself upon the foe. In one of these sallies Frederick captured one of the enemy's soldiers who turned out to be a Cumanian. This fact soon spread through the camp and reached the town where King Kötöny and his army were stationed. Great was the indignation of the Hungarians. They had long hated the Cumanians, suspecting them of being allies of the Tartars sent to Hungary to incite unrest and thus weaken the defence of the country. No attempt was made to verify these rumours. The fact that the Tartars compelled their prisoners to fight for them was ignored. The capture of a Cumanian fighting for the enemy seemed proof positive of their treachery, and the quarters of the Cumanians were stormed and their king killed.

The assassination of Kötöny had dire consequences. Hitherto the Cumanians had regarded themselves as allies of the Hungarians and were willing to support them wholeheartedly. But now they turned against Hungary, and fled the country, vying with the Tartars in sacking towns and villages. They cut their way through towards the regions of the Lower Danube, leaving Béla and his people to their own resources at the time of their greatest need.

In the early days of April the King gave the order to attack. The forces at his disposal, it is said, numbered some 50 or 60 thousand men. This considerable force surprised even Batu Khan, who decided to retreat. The retreat, however, was so cunningly conceived that it not only gave him time enough to rally his scattered troops, but also to choose the most advantageous ground for a pitched battle. This was the hilly land encircled by the rivers Tisza, Hernád and Sajó commanding the flats surrounding Ónod, known as the Puszta of Muhi. There the Tartars, in obedience to their leader's commands, pitched camp and fortified the banks of the river against surprise attacks. The Hungarian forces, close on the heels of the Tartars, came to a halt — just as Batu Khan expected — on the plain of Muhi. They assumed that the Mongols would retreat no farther, and believing themselves on the eve of an engagement, pitched their tents and posted pickets at places likely to serve as fords. The situation of the Hungarian forces was anything but favourable. Their camp was in the plain, and from the hills where the Tartars had pitched their tents Batu Khan and his captains were able to watch every movement of their enemies. Several fatal mistakes had also been made by the Hungarian leaders, who had overlooked the fact that their army, chiefly comprised of mail-clad horsemen, needed large open spaces for battle array, instead of which they were confined in camp, tent close on tent, where movement was greatly restricted. The encampment was surrounded by a stockade of heavy wagons to serve as defence against surprise attacks, but which, in fact, proved an obstacle to a rapid forming of line of battle.

Batu Khan himself is said to have been struck with astonishment at the sight, and to have told his men that victory was certain, for the Hungarians were crowded like sheep in a pen. He decided to open the attack in person and take the enemy by surprise. For several days the two camps seemed on the point of attacking each other. But actually the Tartars were concealing their exploration of points on the rivers Hernád and Sajó where their troops might cross unnoticed and descend unexpectedly upon the Hungarian camp. When they had found and proved the fords they began a series of attacks on the pickets stationed on the banks. The attention of the Hungarians was thus diverted to these points and the manœuvre enabled the entire Tartar forces to cross the rivers and surround the Hungarian camp under cover of night.

Batu Khan's prophecy was fulfilled. The Tartars rained showers of arrows on the Hungarian bivouac, the inmates of which, starting up from their sleep, were quite unable to defend themselves within the narrow confines of the camp. Some, such as Ugrin, the Archbishop of Kalocsa, and the Superior of the Knights Templars, attempted resistance, even to opening a counter-attack, but were both killed. The bulk of the army became panic-stricken and sought safety in flight, only to fall victims to the arrows

71

of the enemy. In a few hours the Hungarian army was completely annihilated and the country at the mercy of a savage and cruel foe. That King Béla escaped was due to an accident and to the self-sacrifice of some loyal followers.

The Tartars did not fail to take full advantage of their victory, and crushing all resistance, they burned and destroyed everything in their advance. The population took refuge in marshes and forests, where they languished in misery, awaiting the hour of deliverance in vain. The King at length rejoined Duke Frederick, who persuaded him, defenceless as he was, to hand over all his gold and even forced him to cede the counties of Moson, Sopron and Vas. Béla determined to shake off this tyrant and speedily left the court of the Duke. Ultimately he found refuge in Dalmatia. The Tartars, taking advantage of the hard winter of 1241—1242 to cross the frozen Danube and pillage the Transdanubian districts, pursued the fugitive King as far as Dalmatia, in an attempt to capture him. But a distant event decreed otherwise. The chief Khan or Emperor of the Tartars died suddenly. Batu Khan, who hoped to succeed him, immediately withdrew his troops from Hungary and returned to his Asiatic home with all haste. Before crossing the Hungarian frontier he ordered the wholesale execution of all the prisoners, whereupon many thousands of Hungarian were cruelly slaughtered.

Béla IV learned from his spies of the departure of the Tartars. At first he was incredulous, but on being assured that the country was rid of its enemies he returned home immediately. Dreadful was the scene awaiting him. Scarcely a living creature was to be seen. Blackened walls and decaying corpses were all that remained of once prosperous villages, no trace of agriculture or farming, and roads had nearly all disappeared. Where they still existed packs of wolves or dogs that had run wild made them unsafe.

The King was torn with grief at the sight of his native land. Before him lay that Hungary which had but recently been a flourishing country, but was now desolated. But Béla was made of tougher stuff than to give way to despair. His first act was to reassemble the scattered population, which had been greatly thinned by famine, and create new settlements for them, providing corn and cattle imported from abroad. Towns were rebuilt, and the townsfolk were permitted to surround their cities with walls. The King bestowed special attention on the construction of fortresses. He had seen that the Tartar onslaughts were powerless against well-fortified strongholds, and it seemed probable that they would renew their invasion. Years of arduous toil were successful in restoring order and peace. Agriculture, handicrafts and trade began to prosper, and the country began to recover slowly from the devastation it had sustained in the years 1241—1242.

Béla IV may justly be named the second builder of the Hungarian Kingdom. The new settlers whom he brought from abroad supported his efforts to reconstruct the country, and in course of time became loyal and useful citizens. Among them we again find the Cumanians, who had begged to be allowed to return, and to prove their loyalty, became converted to the Christian faith. Béla even agreed to the marriage of his son Stephen with the only daughter of King Kötöny, in order to reinforce the friendship between the two races with links of family ties.

When the news of the battle of Muhi and the Tartar scourge reached the western countries, it was generally thought that Hungary had been wiped off the map of Europe. But in 1246, only five years after that battle, Béla IV was again at war, this time with Frederick, Duke of Austria, in order to recover the three counties he had been tricked into ceding to Austria. A battle fought near the Leitha ended in victory for Béla and cost Frederick his life.

Thereafter Hungary was on the way to becoming the most powerful country in Central Europe. Agriculture and cattle-breeding were prospering, towns sprang up in which handicrafts and commerce began to thrive, and along the frontiers and in the interior strongholds were built and garrisoned with well-equipped soldiers. This development was, alas, checked by dissension and quarrels. Béla was a high-handed king who brooked no opposition, much less insubordination. This made him many enemies among the nobility who did not forget that in the reign of Andrew II they had been almost independent oligarchs who could afford to ignore the King's orders. The nobles now began to sow discord and dissension between Béla and his ambitious son Stephen (later Stephen V, 1270—1272), inciting the latter to claim a share in the government of the country. The King, who was growing old, made no objection. He ordered his son to be crowned, allowed him a household and a Palatine of his own, and conferred on him the right to mint money. But this dual monarchy failed to work in practice. The intrigues of evil councillors and their insinuations widened the gulf between father and son until a feud arose between them which put an end to all progress in the country and in many provinces even undid the work already accomplished. In 1270 Béla died, disheartened and disillusioned.

ANDREW III, THE LAST OF THE ÁRPÁD LINE.

1290—1301

The successors of Béla IV. The reign of Ladislas the Cumanian. Decline. Third marriage of Andrew II. Andrew III in Italy. The oligarchs. Coronation of Andrew III. His reign and sudden death.

Under the rule of Béla IV's immediate successors (Stephen V, 1270—1272 ; Ladislas IV or the Cumanian, 1272—1290; Andrew III, 1290—1301) Hungary declined rapidly. The nobles had seized the reins of government, but instead of using their power for the good of the country as a whole, they made it serve their own ends. One factor which at first helped to extend the power of the nobility was that at his accession the King was a minor. The country was ruled by regents and to them the oligarchs refused obedience. The mother of the boy-king was a Cumanian, and Cumanian influences prevailed, not only at Court, but also throughout the country, which was a great source of grievance to the Hungarian nobles. When the King grew to manhood he still clung to the habits and ways of thought of the Cumanians, and spent his time in their company (hence his nick-name "Ladislas the Cumanian"), which completely estranged him from the Hungarians. Yet Ladislas IV had many good qualities. His personal gallantry and strategic ability could not be questioned even by his enemies. On two occasions he gave signal proof of those qualities. Once in 1278, when he took sides with the German Emperor, Rudolph Habsburg, against Ottokar, the powerful King of Bohemia, and helped to gain the victory over the latter which made the creation of the Habsburg dynasty possible. The second occasion was his victory over the turbulent Cumanians at Hódmező-vásárhely. This campaign was undertaken in response to the pleading of the Lords Temporal and Spiritual. Had Ladislas been trained as he should have been and duly prepared for his work as monarch, he might have been one of our best kings, but unfortunately his reign was characterized by general decay and impoverishment. Even decades later, carts drawn by men instead of horses were called "Ladislas carts," a reminder of the fact that during his reign destitution and want had lowered the peasantry to the level of draught horses. The decline of royal authority and the growth of the power and influence of the oligarchs continued even during the reign of the last King of the House of Árpád, Andrew III (1290—1301).

King Andrew II, whose name is famous in its relation to one the most important documents of the Hungarian Constitution, the Golden Bull (of which mention has been made), was an old man when he decided to marry again. His desire to do so was at first regarded with displeasure. His sons feared that were he to remarry and have children internecine wars would result, an evil they wished to avoid at all costs. But the old King, who was longing for the comforts of family life, refused to yield to their entreaties, and in spite of all opposition married an Italian Duchess, Beatrice of Este. The young Queen, who was Andrew's third wife, was coldly received by the King's family, who made no effort to conceal their hostility, and when in the autumn of 1235

KING ANDREW III (1290—1301)
John Thuróczy's Chronicles
(Augsburg, 1488)

Andrew died, she thought it advisable to leave the country with all speed. She returned to Italy, where, at the end of 1235 or the beginning of 1236, she gave birth to a son who was baptized Stephen.

The life of this last descendant of Andrew II was sad and stormy. The fatherless infant seems also to have

77

lost his mother very early, and he became a homeless wanderer at the courts of the Italian Dukes, travelling from town to town. Go to Hungary he dared not, for Béla IV would have nothing to do with him. In Italy therefore he remained. After the death of his first wife he settled down permanently in Venice, and married Thomasina Morosini, a member of one of the most prominent families in the Venetian Republic. Of this marriage was born Andrew, known to Hungarian history as King Andrew III.

This child grew up in the knowledge that he was a legitimate descendant of the Árpáds, and therefore entitled to claim as his patrimony part of the territory of the Hungarian monarchy during the ruling kings's life. This was common usage under the Árpáds, and conditions in the country were favourable to his claim.

After the Tartar invasion Béla IV had set about effecting a reconstruction of the country. As has been said, he built strongholds along the frontiers to serve as places of refuge in times of sudden attack. In order to secure a better defence of the frontiers he also readily consented to the landowners on the borderlands building fortifications and strongholds themselves. This system of border fortification was effective for the time being, but its disadvantages were apparent later when the peace of the country was shattered by the struggle for power between Béla IV and his son, Stephen V. As in every civil war, each side tried to secure as many supporters as possible among the big landowners. The donation of estates proving an effective means of ensuring loyalty, father and son vied with each other in conferring land on those whose assistance they considered important.

At the time of Béla's death in 1270 and his son Stephen's in 1272 there were a number of estates along the frontier from the Adriatic to the Lower Danube whose owners, the oligarchs, were practically minor kings. Some even had standing armies of their own, coined their own money, made war on neighbouring countries and concluded peace without asking the King's consent These unhappy conditions had grown even worse during the minority of Ladislas the Cumanian, son of Stephen V. The oligarchs made no attempt to disguise the fact that they were ready to submit to the King only so long as he connived at their arbitrary lawless behaviour. They immediately turned against him when they saw or thought they saw that he wished to exercise his royal prerogatives. Thereupon the oligarchs took up arms to defend their position and influence even at the cost of civil war. Stephen, and later Andrew, who were anathema at the King's Court, but as descendants of the Árpáds were sure of a warm welcome from the Hungarians, seemed to them likely to be useful tools for that purpose.

As early as 1278 Andrew, supported by the powerful Counts of Németujvár, appeared in the country to lead in person the armed rebellion of the oligarchs in Croatia and the Littoral. Ladislas IV, however, was able to quell the revolt and Andrew had to flee the country. Some years later, when it had become manifestly hopeless to expect the King, who was wholly demoralized and given over to the company of the Cumanians, to mend his ways, certain of the Lords Temporal and Spiritual turned against him and resolved to send for Andrew, whom they believed would reign justly and live with a certain decorum. Andrew accepted their call, but soon realized that the numerous promises made to him before his embarkation on this adventure by no means represented the sentiments, temper and political views of the majority of the population. Only a few rallied to him, and his host, a gentleman named Arnold, hoping for a reward, made him prisoner and carried him to the court of the Austrian Duke Albert, son of Rudolph Habsburg, in Vienna. Albert however behaved with generosity, restored Andrew to liberty and invited him to stay at the Austrian Court. But Andrew did not feel at home and soon took his departure. The immediate reason why he left was as follows: Albert had gone off on a hunting expedition and was absent several days. Some of the courtiers asked Andrew to ride out with them to meet the returning Duke saying that the latter would take it as a mark of respect. Andrew refused, on the plea that by virtue of his origin and race he was of higher rank than his host. The latter, hearing of his refusal, withdrew his protection.

The exiled Prince of the House of Árpád had no choice but to retire to an Austrian monastery. In the seclusion of the monastery news reached him that Ladislas IV was dead (1290), and it was not long before the Archbishop of Esztergom assured Andrew that he was regarded by all as the legitimate heir to the throne, and urged him to return. Andrew, who had taken monastic vows, thereupon left Austria secretly. At the frontier he was received with the greatest honours. Many indeed there were who would have preferred another claimant, but his coronation took place without any untoward incident. This coronation deserves special mention since all the pageantry and ceremonies connected with it have been strictly observed at every coronation down the centuries to the present day. Andrew was the first Hungarian king to take a coronation oath in which he pledged himself to maintain peace and justice, protect the Church, punish evildoers, afford aid to orphans and widows, judge justly according to the laws of the land, defend the country and its rights, and reconquer the dismembered parts of Hungary. These points form the basis of the present coronation oath.

His undisputed coronation and the great interest in its ceremonies displayed all over the country showed that loyalty to and respect for the House of Árpád were alive in the hearts of the people. This was fortunate both for the King and the country, as there were several pretenders who laid claim to the crown on various pretexts, such as Albert of Austria, for instance, the son-in-law of Stephen V, Charles II of Naples, and even the widow of Ladislas IV, who was supported by the Pope. In the face of these claimants royal power had no support other than the loyalty and attachment of the Hungarians and indeed it seemed as if the old reciprocal trust between King and Nation which had been forgotten in the violent party quarrels of the previous decades, had revived again. The Hungarians were united in one camp with Andrew III, and were convinced that the King would take his coronation vows seriously and do his utmost to create order and peace. The King was not an unapproachable man. He went about among his subjects, an embodiment of the law, a rewarder of the good and a chastiser of the wicked. To the people he was a king after their own hearts. Small wonder then that when pretenders to the throne made their appearance with numerous alleged proofs substantiating their claims, all classes and conditions of men in the country rallied round the King, who had become thoroughly Hungarian in sentiment and outlook. Since the Tartar invasion no King had had such a powerful army behind him as Andrew when in the summer of 1291 he opened hostilities against Albert of Austria. The war ended in victory for Andrew, which seemed likely to consolidate his rule.

But his reign was not to be a peaceful one. The oligarchs very soon realized the danger which threatened them as a result of the consolidation of the royal power. Much time and effort on the part of the King were needed to appease and win over the unruly Barons, and there were periods when it seemed doubtful whether Andrew would be able to remain on the throne. However, experience had taught him the advisability of keeping his throne independent of the oligarchs. His policy was distinctly a family one. The most important posts and the administration of the various districts were assigned to members of his own family, in the first place to his energetic and fearless mother and his maternal uncle, and through these channels to reliable Italians. By these means he was able to obtain mastery over the fierce oligarchs, aided by the loyalty which he had won by his justice and fair-dealing from the lesser squires, who looked upon him as their natural and disinterested protector. Through the offices of the Archbishop of Esztergom he also found favour with the Church, of which he constituted himself protector against the predatory oligarchs.

The Royal Family of Naples was determined to secure the crown of Hungary, and the oligarchs jealous for their own waning influence were ready to support the Neapolitans from time to time. On the whole, however, thanks to the energetic assistance afforded by the majority of his subjects, Andrew had every reason to view the future with confidence and satisfaction. But towards the middle of January 1301 — some say on the 14th of that month — he died suddenly. His death, like that of his mother some months earlier, was attributed to poison.

"The last golden branch of the tree of the first Hungarian King, St. Stephen, is broken, the last male descendant of his blood, race and stock is dead ; and the Lords Spiritual and Temporal, the nobility, all classes and ranks of the people feel that Hungary has lost her true-born King and weep for him as Rachel wept for her children."

In these words, uttered two years after the King's death, the Palatine voiced more than a mere private eulogy, they were an expression of the true feelings of the whole Hungarian nation.

KING LOUIS THE GREAT.

1342—1382

The struggle for the Hungarian crown. The Kingdom of Wenceslas and Otto. The rule of Robert Charles. The evolution of Hungary. King Louis' expeditions to Naples and their motives. Conflict with Venice. Louis as King of Poland, National defence. Urban life. The Church.

After Andrew's death the right to elect a king devolved unreservedly upon the nation. Though it was understood by all that only a prince whose mother or grandmother had been a princess of the Árpádian line was eligible, a unanimous election was difficult, since there were three princes who fulfilled that condition. They were Robert Charles, son of Charles Martel, late King of Naples; Wenceslas II, King of Bohemia; and Otto, Duke of Bavaria. Each of course had his own partisans headed by one of the oligarchs. Among the aspirants Charles Robert was the most active. His supporters lived chiefly in the southern or south-western regions. The other parts of the country would have none of him. This active Prince was actually crowned in haste at Esztergom by the Primate, but not with St. Stephen's crown. Disregarding this coronation, the greater part of the country in response to the suggestion made by Matthias Csák, one of the most powerful oligarchs in the north-west, took sides with King Wenceslas and elected his son of the same name King of Hungary. This young King, however, turned out to be a ruler of questionable worth. He is said to have been a drunkard. His supporters soon deserted him, and his father found it wise to recall him to Prague. On the way home he sacked Esztergom and carried St. Stephen's crown away with him. Otto, Duke of Bavaria, now became Csák's candidate, and he was duly elected, but without the assent of the powerful Voivode of Transylvania. When the new King paid the Voivode a visit with the intention of asking his daughter in marriage in order to win his support, the Voivode seized him and kept him prisoner for several years. After his release Otto decided to return to Bavaria.

Like a ripe fruit the crown fell into the hands of Robert Charles. The majority of the population were anxious for peace and order after years of war and suffering. They elected him King in 1308, only Matthias Csák and a few other oligarchs protesting. But the King had need of all his wits and endurance before he reduced the malcontents to submission. Alone Matthias Csák

LOUIS THE GREAT, KING OF HUNGARY

Képes Krónika XIV
National Museum

remained irreconcilable and until his death led a wild, lawless life in his fastness at Trencsén.

The reign of Robert Charles (1308—1342) proved a blessing to the country. He restored internal order and strengthened the royal authority. Hungary became a peaceful, law-abiding country. Marketing, husbandry, cattle-breeding, and trade in general once again flourished. Economic progress was greatly furthered by the circulation of the excellent gold and silver money coined by the King. His Hungarian money was gladly accepted at its face value even in foreign countries. The King devoted special attention to the defence of his kingdom, which he completely reorganized, compelling every landowner to maintain a number of soldiers recording to the size his estate. No wonder that the fame of a Hungary financially solvent and strong from a military point of view increased, and that the European Powers vied with one another for the favour of an alliance with her. The King of Naples was proud to give his daughter in marriage to the King's younger son Andrew and to make him his heir, and the King of Poland, grateful for the assistance repeatedly rendered by the King of Hungary against the pagan Lithuanians and Tartars, pronounced his elder son Louis heir to the childless King Casimir. Robert Charles was asked on one occasion to act as arbiter in a dispute between Poland and Bohemia, and settled the matter to the complete satisfaction of both parties. On his death (1342) his son Louis (1342—1382) inherited a kingdom well-ordered, powerful and wealthy and playing a leading rôle in Eastern Europe.

Louis known to history as "The Great," was fully conscious of the magnitude of the task falling to him. He was a true Hungarian and wished for nothing better than to be the beloved king of a happy country. He desired to be in every respect worthy of the cloak of St. Ladislas, the glory of whose reign was still a living memory in the country. When Louis' coronation had taken place he felt impelled to go on a pilgrimage to the tomb of that saint and king and there to make a vow to model his conduct as ruler on that of St. Ladislas. And in piety, humanity and courage he, of all the kings of Hungary, was the most worthy to be that great King's successor.

During the first years of his reign he was often forced to wage war, but never without good reason. He never shed Hungarian blood unless circumstances compelled him. Whenever he could do so without jeopardizing Hungary's prestige, he was the first to extend his hand in token of peace. But where energy and determination were necessary he was hard and unyielding. Louis' first campaign was against the Kingdom of Naples. Mention has already been made of the agreement concluded between Robert Charles and the King of Naples by which the Neapolitan crown was promised to Louis' younger brother Andrew. But this agreement irritated the Italians, for though Robert Charles was of Italian origin, and probably spoke faulty Hungarian, he and his family were regarded as aliens in Italy — foreigners who were not wanted on the Neapolitan throne. The King of Naples dared not act against public opinion. Arbitrarily cancelling the agreement with Robert Charles he drew up a will making his only daughter Johanna heir to the throne. Her husband Andrew, to whom she had been married several years, had perforce to content himself with a minor Duchy. After the death of the King of Naples Andrew was cut off from the succession. He was in fact treated so harshly that he went in fear of his life at that intriguing, degenerate Court, above all when even his wife Johanna turned against him and joined his enemies. On learning of his intolerable position, King Louis at once sent his mother, the dowager Queen Elizabeth, to Naples to investigate the true situation and act accordingly. Johanna and her Court were anything but pleased to see Queen Elizabeth, but they received her with much apparent kindness and went so far to meet her wishes that she returned to Hungary completely reassured, especially when after prolonged negotiations the Pope decreed that Andrew was to be crowned King of Naples.

Great, however, was the consternation of Andrew's enemies when they heard the Papal decision. Fearing Andrew's vengeance when he became King they decided to make away with him before the coronation could take place. Fate favoured their sinister plans. The Royal Court was hunting in the neighbourhood of a town called Aversa. Andrew's enemies were all present. After the chase the royal huntsman and his retinue put up for the night in a castle near the town. Under cover of darkness, in the small hours of the morning, the conspirators induced Andrew on some pretext to leave his chamber. As there was a superstitious belief that neither iron nor poison could harm him, they strangled him and flung his corpse into the castle garden. Johanna, who was well aware of what was happening listened to the sounds of the struggle between her husband and his assassins, but made no effort to save him. She attempted later to exonerate herself by professing to have been under the influence of a spell which made her powerless to prevent the crime (1345).

The news of Prince Andrew's murder spread rapidly through Europe. The Royal Court of Hungary was in a ferment of horror and indignation. King Louis bitterly resented the cruel murder of his brother, and decided to inflict dire punishment on the perpetraters of this gross insult and injury to his family. For a time, in the hope that the Pope would pronounce sentence on the evil-doers he paused, but when no condemnation was forthcoming, he declared war on Naples. Johanna escaped to France, and when the news of her flight leaked out in Naples the city offered but feeble resistance and soon surrendered. Louis meted out severe punishment to the instigators of this dastardly crime. He adopted the title of "King of Jerusalem and Sicily," and was considering having himself crowned King of Naples, when the plague that had broken out in Italy shortly before compelled him to return home (May 1348). But he left Hungarian garrisons in possession of Naples and other Italian towns.

The conquest of Naples, however, did not prove permanent. A national movement incited by Johanna and her followers broke out among the Italian population against Louis and his Hungarian rule. To the Italians the Hungarians were alien conquerors, and their proud spirit would not submit to domination by strangers. After King Louis' departure the Neapolitans rallied round Johanna, who had meanwhile been recalled, and they assisted her to retake the Italian strongholds held by the Hungarians. The latter, who had meanwhile received reinforcements, fought with great bravery, but the King, who appeared at the head of an army under the walls of Naples (1350), could not but realize that his grip on Italian soil would depend entirely on force of arms This, being furthermore but a precarious hold, would put Hungary to enormous and perhaps unnecessary expense, and when the Papal See promised that justice should be done, he returned to Hungary and withdrew his forces from Italy.

The two Neapolitan expeditions were undertaken more in the interests of the Royal Family than of the nation, and were indeed productive of no tangible advantage to the country, yet they brought King Louis and the nation nearer to each other. The King proved an excellent commander and a gallant soldier. He shared the privations and discomforts of camp with his soldiers, lived with them, and rewarded liberally those who were deserving. He was as careful of the lives of others as he was reckless of his own. When one of his soldiers, who had been ordered to explore a ford for the army was attempting to cross the river, he was carried away horse and all by the current. Upon seeing this, the King himself plunged without hesitation into the torrent and saved the man from drowning. With such an example before them the soldiers could not but honour their King.

King Louis' wars did not cease with the end of the Neapolitan campaigns. For several decades he was at war with the powerful and wealthy Venetian Republic, which at that time almost entirely controlled European trade. The war with Venice was undertaken in order to gain possession of Dalmatia and secure an outlet on the Adriatic for Hungarian trade. Venice, whose material resources were at stake, stubbornly defended her interests, but was eventually obliged to conclude peace (1381) and pledge herself to pay an annual tribute to Hungary.

As the ally of King Casimir, Louis also waged war on the Tartars, Lithuanians, and Bohemians. He forced the Prince of Serbia and the Wallachian Voivode to surrender, and enlarged the territory of the Hungarian Kingdom by the conquest of Bosnia and Bulgaria. It is not a matter for surprise that after Casimir's death the Poles elected him King of Poland (1370), or that when the Turks appeared in Europe and the idea of a great crusade against them began to spread throughout the Christian countries at the appeal of the Pope, Louis was considered by the European monarchs as the leader who might bring victory to the Christian forces. Alas for Hungary, nothing came of the proposed crusade and subsequently for more than three hundred years she was compelled to wage a struggle to the death alone against the Turk, in which innumerable lives and untold wealth were lost. How different might Hungary's position have been today had she not been bled white in protecting Europe from the hordes of Osman!

It was his martial achievements that earned for Louis the title of "the Great," although his greatness was also manifest in times of peace. With an eye to the distant future, he did not neglect the present. On his journeys through neighbouring countries he came to realize that the Hungarians were a race apart in the Danube Valley and that, isolated and surrounded on all sides by alien and hostile races, the integrity of Árpád's heritage depended entirely on their own efforts and the cultivation of a higher standard of civilization.

In 1351, after the first Neapolitan compaign Louis had several laws enacted by the Estates of the Realm dealing with the organization of the country's defence and the obligations of the nobility. (Nobility in Hungarian law meant all who were not serfs.) In his opinion the nobility had but one duty — to defend the country, but that duty was imperative. It must be remembered that in those times the peasants all over Europe were serfs. In Hungary the serfs were not obliged to serve in the army. To the nobles therefore also fell the task of protecting the farms of the peasantry. The one class had to fight, the other to toil. But the military obligations of the nobility cost them a great deal, expecially during lengthy wars, and to provide them with means for the defence of the country, a law was passed laying a tax on the farms of the serfs, who had to pay one-ninth. The nobles were exempt from taxation. This was quite in keeping with the spirit of the age nor was it considered an injustice by the serfs, who saw that the National Assembly protected their interests and rights in other respects.

Another law enacted in 1351 by the Estates of the Realm, the so-called Law of Entail, dealt with the military obligations of the nobles. To understand this law we must bear in mind the Golden Bull and the Law laid down by Robert Charles which compelled the nobles to maintain a certain number of soldiers, corresponding with the size of their estates. As the Golden Bull gave every nobleman unrestricted rights over his property, so that he could sell it or give it away at his pleasure, it frequently happened that in the course of time these estates were broken up into small holdings which fell into the hands of strangers. In this way the large estates gradually ceased to exist, and the obligation to supply the King with soldiers ceased with them. The Law laid down by Robert Charles would not have attained its object except in cases where the sale or donation of an estate was for some reason or other impossible, and the permanent possession thereof by the same family assured. To meet King Louis' wishes this problem was settled in 1351 by the Estates of the Realm in such a manner that the unrestricted rights of noblemen over their property as

KING LOUIS THE GREAT (1342—1382)
John Thuróczy's Chronicles (Augsburg, 1488)

embodied in the Golden Bull were abolished and a law passed by which ancestral estates could neither be cut up or given away, but must for ever remain the property of the same families. Should a family die out the entailed land reverted to the Crown, became state property, and was entirely at the disposal of the King.

This Law ensuring the integrity of ancestral property remained in force until 1848. In the first half of the past century Count Stephen Széchenyi, one of the greatest statesmen Hungary has produced, fought against it as a superfluous relic of the past and a hindrance to economic development. By Széchenyi's day that was as true as the fact that the Law fulfilled its purpose for centuries and was to a great extent instrumental in keeping the soil of Hungary in Hungarian hands.

During the Neapolitan and Venetian wars Louis had ample opportunity of studying life in the Italian cities. He saw that they were flourishing centres of industry and trade, where also the sciences and arts found ready supporters. They vied with one another, not alone in hoarding wealth within their walls, but also in creating the outward signs of prosperity. Every town boasted magnificent public buildings and churches adorned with paintings and statues of great value. Artists, poets and scientists were treated with great deference, for the citizens felt that the monuments, pictures, poetry, schools, and libraries would proclaim to posterity their love of culture. Nor were they mistaken. Today, as in the past, hundreds of thousands come from the four quarters of the world to delight in the art treasures that have accumulated in Italy down the centuries.

Louis the Great also came under the spell of the wealth and beauty of those cities. He was eager to encourage urban life in Hungary and raise its standard of civilization in general. To that end he encouraged the building of towns by granting them various privileges and indemnities. He promoted the development of handicrafts and trade and had excellent roads constructed.

As the wealth of the citizens grew he began to urge the erection of public buildings, the foundation of schools and hospitals, and the patronage of the arts. The King himself set a good example by building beautiful castles at his favourite resorts, such as Buda, Visegrád, and Diósgyőr. A university was founded at Pécs and a magnificent Gothic church built in Kassa.

He was very generous to the Church. Deeply religious, he took pleasure in building churches, visiting shrines, and reading pious books. When fatigued by the cares of government or exhausted from fighting, he would retire into solitude and seek recreation in pious contemplation and religious exercises. His attachment to the Church inspired him with the idea of trying to draw the neighbouring nations into the fold of the Roman Catholic faith. He set about this task with the conviction that the removal of religious barriers between the Hungarians and their neighbours (the Serbs, Bosnians, Wallachians, and Bulgarians) would lead to more intimate political relations. His efforts, however, were more or less abortive. The peoples of the Balkan Peninsula remained faithful to the Oriental Church and regarded Louis not as a disinterested Catholic monarch, but as the King of Hungary, the ruler of a country which menaced their national characteristics. This was also the reason why Hungary could never rely on the help of the Serbs and Wallachians in her wars against the Turk. Louis died in 1382 at Nagyszombat. In accordance with his last wishes he was laid to rest in Nagyvárad by the side of St. Ladislas.

JOHN HUNYADI, REGENT OF HUNGARY.

(† 1456)

John Hunyadi's origin. The Turkish invasion. Sigismund's reign. Struggles for the throne after the death of King Albert. Hunyadi as Ban of Szörény, Voivode of Transylvania, and Captain of Nándorfehérvár (Belgrade). The reign of Wladislas I. Hunyadi's victories over the Turks. The battle of Várna and Wladislas' death. Hunyadi, Regent of Hungary. Ladislas V. The victory of Belgrade. Hunyadi's death. Ladislas V and the House of Hunyadi. Matthias elected King.

The enemies of Hungary accuse us of having oppressed the non-Hungarian speaking nationalities, of having checked their development and made self-expression impossible for them. This accusation is easily disproved. We have but to point to the Saxons in Transylvania and Sepusia who, though far from numerous, were able for more than seven hundred years to preserve both their language and habits, increase their wealth and make progress in civilization. Or take the Swabian, Slovak and Serb villagers in the vicinity of Budapest. Though living close to the capital for two hundred years they have never even learned the language of the country properly and suffer no loss or disability in consequence. Actually the Hungarians have always been tolerant towards those of alien race and tongue in their midst. Nothing was ever expected of them but loyalty to the country which adopted them and gave them their daily bread.

The case of John Hunyadi also proves that in Hungary foreign origin has never been a hindrance to the

acquisition of wealth and power. The descendants of
non-Hungarian families resident in Hungary have not
only become members of the Hungarian nobility, but
have also risen according to their deserts, to the highest
positions in the land. John Hunyadi's father, Vajk,

KING SIGISMUND,
KING OF HUNGARY AND EMPEROR
OF GERMANY (1395—1437)
John Thuróczy's Chronicles (Augsburg, 1488)

immigrated with his parents from Wallachia to Hungary,
where he became one of King Sigismund's bodyguards.
In 1409, for his loyal service, he received from the King
the castle of Vajda-Hunyad with its adjoining estates.
At the same time by Letters Patent the family took the

name of Hunyadi. John Hunyadi came to the court of the King as a youth and was one of Sigismund's favourites, accompanying him on his numerous journeys to foreign countries. A study of life in the Catholic countries of the west and many years at the Royal Court effected a complete change in the youth. He joined the Catholic Church and became Hungarian in his feelings. The change is not difficult to understand if we remember that his mother and his wife, Elizabeth Szilágyi, were both Hungarian by birth. All his life he fought for Hungary, and we are thoroughly justified in considering him one of her greatest national heroes, like Louis the Great, who, though his father Robert Charles was born in Italy — and we do not even know that he spoke Hungarian well — was a true Hungarian.

John Hunyadi's name became famous throughout Europe through his wars against the Turks. As soon as they had gained a foothold in Europe the Turks began to overrun the Balkan Peninsula. The Christian countries of the west immediately realized that they were confronted by a new and serious danger. Of the once mighty Byzantine Empire scarcely anything remained beyond the capital, Constantinople, which was being more and more hard pressed by the Turks. One after another the Infidels had conquered the countries of the Balkans, and when in 1389 they subdued the Serbs, the way to the Danube stood open. The defeat of the Serbs and the tidings that the Turks had crossed the Danube and were on Hungarian soil filled the European nations with alarm. They felt that the Christian world of the west was seriously threatened with the danger of being overrun by the Infidels. If the growth of Turkish power could not be checked in time, it was evident that later all efforts to do so would fail. In response to the Pope's appeal a large international army was recuited in the western states, but in 1396 it was annihilated at Nicapolis, and Hungary was left to defend herself as best she could.

It was unfortunate for Hungary that Sigismund, the husband of Louis the Great's elder daughter Maria and by virtue thereof King of the Hungarians, became also Emperor of Germany in 1410. From that year he was solely concerned with the affairs of the German Empire, the Bohemian wars, and the crisis which had arisen within the Catholic Church. These troubles kept him away from Hungary for years at a time and the years spent abroad served to estrange the Hungarians from Sigismund. Among his frequent journeys in foreign lands he also visited England. On this occasion he concluded a formal treaty in Canterbury with Henry V. Sigismund was an ardent admirer of England. On his return he was loud in his praises of the excellency of English government and declared that it was as if he had been in Paradise (ut quasi essem in Paradiso). Ties of blood and friendship linked him with contemporary English monarchs.

Although the Turkish menace was growing increasingly threatening, King Sigismund had little time to devote to the task of averting it. It 1428 the stronghold of Galambóc on the Danube fell thanks to Serb treachery, and the Turks gained a footing on the Hungarian frontier. In vain did King Sigismund try to recover this important frontier fortress. In an attempt to do so he suffered such a shattering defeat that it was all he could do to escape with his life. He died in 1437.

His son-in-law Albert, who was also heir to the German Imperial crown succeeded him (1437—1439). During his short reign, Semendria, another important Hungarian fortress on the Lower Danube, passed into the possession of the Turks. Hoping to avoid further disasters Albert appointed John Hunyadi Ban of Szörény

HUNGARIAN XV CENTURY COSTUMES

(A picture embroidered on silk)
Vestry of the Aachen Dome

(1439). During Sigismund's wars Hunyadi had more than once given splendid proof of his strategical ability, and this was why he was entrusted with the defence of the southern frontier. As things were, Hunyadi's appointment was a stroke of good luck for Hungary, for King Albert died and there was no one to rule the country at the moment when a fresh Turkish onslaught was pending. The nation split into two camps over the question of the vacant throne. The widowed Queen claimed the crown for her infant son Ladislas and set about winning a large party of adherents in the country. In view of the imminent danger of a Turkish invasion others, Hunyadi among them, advocated the election of a king who would be a military asset and would add his own personal prestige to that of the country. This party offered the crown to Wladislas, King of Poland, who accepted it. Meanwhile the Queen-dowager had her infant son crowned. Thus there were two Kings of Hungary backed by parties strongly opposed to each other. Those who had the future of the country and not their own private interests at heart tried in vain to effect a compromise. Their efforts suffered shipwreck on the rock of a mutual hatred that was stronger than patriotism, and civil war broke out when nearly all the forts on the borders were in the hands of the Turks who were preparing to attack.

In these desperate straits it was nothing short of providential that King Wladislas made John Hunyadi Ban of Szörény, Voivode of Transylvania and Captain of Belgrade (1440). By doing so he placed the defence of the southern frontier, the region most exposed to danger, in the hands of one single leader. The Turks were quick to notice the radical change in the military situation.

Hunyadi remained aloof from the civil strife in which even foreigners, chiefly Czechs (Bohemians), who were the Queen's hirelings took sides, and devoted himself entirely to his military duties. In 1441 he succeeded in inflicting a crushing blow on some Turkish bands who had crossed the Danube and were looting southern Hungary. This reverse made them hesitate to cross the Danube again for a long time. Instead they advanced on Transylvania: confident that there they would encounter no resistance and that rich booty would fall into their hands.

In the spring of 1442 a powerful Turkish army entered Transylvania under the command of Mezit Beg. Hunyadi with the small force at his disposal advanced at once against the enemy. His troops joined forces with the army of George Lépes, Bishop of Transylvania, and fought a losing battle against the superior numbers of the Turks. The Bishop fell on the battlefield fighting heroically and Hunyadi himself barely managed to make his escape. Defeat, however, did not discourage him from attacking again. Hearing that the Turks were laying siege to Nagyszeben (Hermanstadt) he recruited an army from among the Siculian and Hungarian population and joining the forces of his co-Voivode, Nicolas de Ujlak, hurried to the relief of the town. Some Turkish prisoners had brought tidings that Mezit Beg was determined at all costs to take Hunyadi, dead or alive, and that he had issued commands to that effect. Hearing this, a gallant Hungarian knight, Simon Kemény by name, begged Hunyadi to change horses and armour with him and let him ride at the head of a squadron of knights into the centre of the Turkish attack. Meanwhile Hunyadi was to outflank the enemy and attack in the rear. If this ruse succeeded victory would be assured. Hunyadi at first refused but later agreed and changed horses and armour with Simon Kemény. The Turks fell with savage ferocity upon the troops at whose head they thought to find Hunyadi, and broke into a roar of triumph when they saw the leader fall. They now confidently expected that the army, deprived of its leader would turn and flee. But at the critical moment Hunyadi, who had meanwhile outflanked the Turks, fiercely attacked, and the besieged garrison made a desperate sally. The Turks on learning that Hunyadi was alive and at the head of the army were panic-stricken, and fled. After the battle the bodies of twenty thousand Turks covered the field, that of Mezit Beg among them. Many prisoners and much booty were taken. As a result of Mezit Beg's defeat at Nagyszeben the Wallachian Voivodes withdrew their alliegance from the Sultan and once more recognized the suzerainty of Hungary. This roused the wrath of the Sultan, who in the summer of the same year sent yet another army to Transylvania. Hunyadi routed it near Karánsebes, near the Iron Gates of the Danube.

The news of these two victories spread all over Europe. Hunyadi was regarded as a God-sent leader who would assure the victory of the Christian armies. Hunyadi appealed to the Christian powers to unite as speedily as possible and make a concentrated attack on the Turks. But his appeal met with scarcely any response. Only Hungary, encouraged by his victories, decided to take the offensive under King Wladislas. Fighting began in July 1443 and lasted till February 1444. The Hungarians crossed the Danube and advanced through Sophia towards the mountains of the Balkans. They wiped out several smaller Turkish armies, took many prisoners and captured much booty.

The psychological effect of this successful campaign was important. It was the first time after several decades of purely defensive warfare that Hungary opened hostilities herself, and with splendid results. Rumours were in circulation that Germany, Venice and other European powers were making ready to join Hungary in striking a decisive blow at the enemies of Christianity. Encouraged by promises received from the Papal Nuncio Julianus, the Estates of the Realm resolved to continue the war. At that time Wladislas and his court were in Szeged. The Sultan's emissaries appeared at the Court and in their master's name proposed peace on acceptable terms. Acting on the advice of his councillors, King Wladislas concluded peace with the Sultan in July 1444. The King and the Estates were now in an awkward predicament. Those who did not believe in the sincerity of the Sultan argued in favour of a new offensive. Their arguments were supported by the fact that the Sultan had left unfulfilled certain conditions of the treaty. Finally the war party gained the upper hand and after much serious thought Wladislas decided to accede to their demands.

The army which marched on the enemy consisted of scarcely 20.000 men, which were obviously not sufficient to achieve great results. But the Hungarians relied upon the promised assistance of the other countries and that the main body of the Sultan's army would be preoccupied in Asia. They also hoped that the fleets cruising in the Straits would blockade that route and therefore they would be able to achieve the object of the campaign and drive the Turks out of Europe. Alas! All these hopes were doomed to dissapointment. The western States failed them. The Sultan, on hearing that the Hungarians were on the march hurriedly concluded peace in Asia and returned to the European battle-ground. The European fleets in the Straits could not prevent the passage of the Turkish forces, the less so as the latter moved secretly, and with remarkable speed. It was only on November 9th, under the walls of Várna, that the Hungarians learned of the close proximity of the Sultan's army, which was encamped but a short distance off.

After prolonged deliberation the Hungarian council of war decided to attack the Turks, although they outnumbered the Hungarians several times over. The battle began next day under circumstances that seemed to promise victory. Hunyadi routed the Turkish mounted troops and was already close on the heels of the Sultan. Then King Wladislas thinking victory was certain and fearful lest Hunyadi should get all the credit for it, threw his own forces upon the hitherto unbroken ranks of Turkish infantry, the Janissaries. After a fierce struggle the Turks were victorious and nearly the whole of Wladislas' army was wiped out, the King himself being among the slain.

His death paralyzed the Hungarians, who wavered and began to break. In vain Hunyadi tried to rally his troops, but the battle was lost and Hunyadi himself was compelled to flee for his life.

As is usual when disaster overtakes an army the most conflicting rumours arose throughout the country. Nothing certain was known concerning the fate of the King, Hunyadi and the Papal Nuncio. Finally, it was established that Hunyadi escaped death but was taken prisoner by the Voivode of Wallachia, who, fearing the Sultan's revenge and wishing to appease him, proposed handing Hunyadi over to the Turks. At the urgent request, however, of the Hungarian Estates, Hunyadi was liberated.

His return helped, but only partially, to clear up the situation. That the Papal Nuncio had been killed on the field seemed certain, but where was Wladislas? Many asserted that he had escaped. This did not seem impossible, for in 1396, after the battle of Nicapolis, King Sigismund had shown no sign of life for months. Until, therefore, the King returned, the Estates placed the reins of government in the hands of five commanders or captains — Hunyadi among them. But this did not work well, and when the King's death was more or less certain, Hunyadi suggested that Albert's son Ladislas should ascend the throne, and that during his minority the country be ruled by a regent elected by the Estates with an advisory council to support him. The diet of the Estates, which met on the plain of Rákos, adopted this motion, and with great enthusiasm elected Hunyadi Regent of Hungary with almost royal prerogatives (1446).

Hunyadi's regency lasted six years. During that time he had to contend with the jealousy of many rivals, who did their best to put stumbling-blocks in his path. This is why he could not boast of many outstanding achievements. Thanks to the treachery of the Wallachians, who went over to the enemy, he suffered defeat at Rigómező in 1448. Nevertheless, his regency was fortunate for the country, since he checked the general decadence that had set in. His success in this direction was certainly in part due to the fact that he was able to organize a large army of volunteers. Under his rule the army ceased to be a haphazard militia dependent on the mood of the nobility. It became a well-equipped and disciplined regular army, and one of the best in Europe at that.

In 1452 he handed the country over to Ladislas V (1452—1457), who had now grown to manhood. Ladislas, as a token of his gratitude, appointed Hunyadi commander-in-chief of the army and thus the defence of the country fortunately remained in the same hands.

The young King had been brought up under the guardianship of his uncle Ulric Czilley, who educated the youth as if all a king needed to know was to dance and enjoy himself. He also poisoned the mind of the young King by making him jealous of John Hunyadi and his family, and filled him with distrust of the Hungarian nation as a whole. Thanks to this the unfortunate young King avoided Hungary and spent most of his time in Vienna or Prague among Germans and Bohemians. It is not difficult to guess what would have become of Hungary or of indolent Europe had the defence of the country been in the hands of Ladislas V, instead of in those of Hunyadi, at a time when the hordes of Islam were again preparing to attack.

In 1453 Constantinople fell and the thousand-year-old Greek Empire passed for ever from the map of Europe. The new Sultan, Mohammed, openly proclaimed his intention of subjugating Europe. By 1454 his armies were on the banks of the Danube, ready to advance, when the fortresses had been taken, on Hungary. Hunyadi's alertness and courage, however, averted the danger. But the Sultan was not to be deterred from a second attempt. He assembled a great army and decided to lead it in person against Belgrade, then considered the key to Hungary. His huge preparations roused the anxiety of all the Christian nations of Europe. On learning of the Sultan's intentions, Hunyadi first put the stronghold of Belgrade in a state of preparedness, duly garrisoned it and entrusted his son-in-law Michael Szilágyi and his own son Ladislas with its defence. He himself set about reinforcing the army. In this he was greatly assisted by John Kapisztrán, a Franciscan monk and an enthusiastic advocate of the union of the Christian nations against the Turks. His ardent and impassioned speeches induced a powerful host of crusaders to join Hunyadi's army at Szeged, which advanced to the relief of Belgrade, by that time sorely pressed both by land and river. Hunyadi first scattered the Turkish boats and then penetrated into the city.

The relieving troops arrived in the nick of time. Shortly after their arrival the Sultan ordered the town to be carried by storm. At first the Turks managed to force an entrance, but after a fierce struggle the counter-attack of the crusaders forced them to retire. Fired by this success, the Hungarians fell on the Turkish camp and captured it with its provisions and guns. The enemy fled leaving thousands of dead on the field, and the Sultan himself was wounded and barely escaped being made prisoner.

Hunyadi's victory was overwhelming. The defeat sustained by the Turks was so crushing that Belgrade and its environs were safe from them for the next seventy years. When the glad news spread, the success of the Christian armies was celebrated everywhere by the Christian peoples, who felt that they had been saved from the Turkish yoke. In commemoration of that victory the Pope celebrated masses and ordered the church bells to be rung at noon throughout the Christian world. In Oxford the fall of Nándorfehérvár (Belgrade) was also welcomed — as we read in the history of the Oxford University — with a peal of bells and great celebrations. It is interesting to note that Hunyadi sent a special courier, Erasmus Fullar, to Oxford with the news of the victory. The custom still exists even among Protestant, Greek Catholic and Orthodox congregations, but Hungary's service to Christian civilization, of which it was intended to be a reminder, has been more or less forgotten.

Hungary paid a very heavy price for this victory. The plague which broke out among the troops first carried off John Hunyadi on 11th August 1456, and some days later John Kapisztrán, who was afterwards canonized by the Catholic Church. Their memory is still revered in Hungary.

Ladislas V and his entourage held completely aloof from the deep national mourning which followed the great hero's death. Who knows? Perhaps they even rejoiced in their hearts, for Czilley and others of like mind had always refused to see anything more than an envied and hated rival in Hunyadi, whom to their chagrin they had been powerless to harm. Personal enemies of Hunyadi and his family, they counted on the indifference and weakness of the young King and judged the moment favourable to seize control and break up the party that had been supporting the great Captain. They reckoned well. Ladislas V appointed Czilley chief military commander of the country and ordered Ladislas Hunyadi, who expected to receive the post, to hand over all the fortresses entrusted to him by his father. The King then went to Belgrade to inspect the battlefield, and took Czilley with him in his new capacity. Ladislas Hunyadi admitted the King and his Hungarian followers into the fortress, but invoking the constitutional laws of the country, refused to allow the German mercenaries to follow him. It may have been through this, or perhaps as an outcome of the new commander's arrogant behaviour, that a bitter controversy arose between Ladislas Hunyadi and Czilley. The former reproached Czilley for his duplicity and hostility which had wrought so much evil on the country. The war of words soon developed into a fight with swords, Hunyadi's followers intervened and Czilley was killed.

Terrified by his uncle's unhappy end Ladislas V accepted the explanations of Hunyadi and his friends, but could not be brought to admit that Czilley was guilty of the charges laid against him. Surrounded, however, by the henchmen of the Hunyadis he pretended to condone by-gones and be willing to respect ancient traditions. As proof of his good faith he appointed Ladislas Hunyadi military commander of the country, and returning home, swore to Elizabeth Szilágyi not to seek revenge for Czilley's death. But on reaching Buda he changed his mind. At the Court there was no one who was not a sworn enemy of the Hunyadi's. His courtiers easily succeeded in fanning the flames of the King's smouldering wrath. All argued that the assassination of Czilley had been deliberate, the authors of it wishing to make away with the most powerful and trustworthy of the King's supporters prior to seizing the crown. According to opinion at Court, the King, if he wished to avert a catastrophe, could do no less than exterminate the Hunyadis and their party, root and branch. Ladislas, brought up to hate the Hunyadis, was inclined to believe what he was told. He had no personal objection to arresting the two young men with some of their more influential supporters and arraigning them before the courts of justice as traitors to King and country. The tribunal, composed of enemies of the family, condemned them to death without a hearing and ordered the confiscation of their estates. The sentence of death pronounced on Ladislas Hunyadi was executed on 16th March 1457 on St. George's Square in Buda in the King's presence. The others were imprisoned. When it became known that Ladislas Hunyadi had been beheaded, a revolution broke out. At the head of it was Michael Szilágyi. The squires in particular flocked to his standard and turned furiously against all who were suspected of being on the King's side and enemies of the Hunyadis. General indignation was so strong that the King thought it wise to leave the country. He established his Court first in Vienna, then in Prague, and wherever he went he carried his prisoner, Matthias Hunyadi, with him. But it was not long before Ladislas V was called to his account before a Higher tribunal. He died on 13th November 1457, after a few days illness as he was contemplating marriage. He was one of the Hungarian Kings who have left the most tragic memories behind them — a men condemned from birth to be a constant provoker of strife and feuds.

After his death the chief question for the nation to decide was once again that of the succession. There was no lack of aspirants. But the overwhelming majority of the nation joined in an electioneering campaign with the name of Matthias Hunyadi on their lips. The Diet of Electors consisting of the nobility and gentry held their first session in Pest at the beginning of January 1458. It soon transpired that not only the squires but also the majority of the aristocracy were in favour of Matthias, and that there was no serious obstacle to his election. The debate, nevertheless, lasted for weeks, and the electors assembled in the city began to get impatient. On January 23rd a crowd of squires and citizens gathered on the ice of the frozen Danube and began to cheer Matthias. The response to this demonstration was so spontaneous and public opinion so unanimous that the Diet as one man proclaimed Matthias King of Hungary. With due regard to his youth they elected a Regent in the person of Michael Szilágyi. The news of his election to the throne was conveyed by a delegation to Matthias in Prague, where the young Hunyadi had just recovered his liberty after Ladislas' death. The same delegation accompanied him on his way home. His journey was a veritable triumph, for his election was regarded as the victory of right and justice over tyranny, and the welcome was correspondingly warm.

KING MATTHIAS.

*Monument of King Matthias in Kolozsvár by John Fadrusz.
The Turkish wars of King Matthias. His European
alliance against the Turks. His ambition to be Emperor of
Germany. His wars for the Bohemian crown. His standing
army. Economic life in Hungary. Matthias as a Maecenas
of science and art.*

The traveller who after a somewhat lengthy journey
from Budapest arrives in Kolozsvár, the former capital
of Transylvania, should stop and see a fine statue of King
Matthias standing before the old Gothic church of St.
Michael's. The monument is the work of a great artist.
It combines strength and creative force with an expression
of the tender regard and admiration felt for Matthias
Hunyadi by the whole Hungarian nation. The King
on horseback, in full armour, stands on a bastion and
seems content with his achievements. At the foot of
the statue the King's captains proudly display the colours
of the conquered countries. The statue, which is the
work of John Fadrusz, stands in the principle square of
Kolozsvár, not far from the house were on 22nd February
1440 Matthias was born. The sculptor has managed
to convey an adequate idea of King Matthias's impressive
personality. Since the days of St. Ladislas no Hungarian
King has left such an indelible impression on the country,
and the memory of no other has been so reverently
preserved as his. Centuries have passed, but the proverbs
which tell of his love of justice and fair dealing are still
fresh on the lips of the people, and throughout the long

and stormy periods which have since elapsed his memory has been greatly instrumental in sustaining the faith of the nation in a better future. Yet his reign was anything but peaceful, as the standard-bearers at the foot of his monument testify. This was not because he loved warfare, but because the spirit of the age and the state of Central Europe made it inevitable. The inheritance left by John Hunyadi was to continue the struggle against the Turks. The first years of his reign were spent in a continuous battling against the Turkish Crescent in wars that again and again proved him the worthy successor of his father. Christendom acclaimed him as a God-sent champion whose mission was to solve Europe's direst problem — the expulsion of the Turk from European soil.

The experience gained in long years of warfare taught Matthias that Hungary alone was not powerful enough to crush the great military machine of a Turkish Empire so much richer in resources than herself. Only an all-embracing European alliance could, in his opinion, carry on the struggle with any prospect of success. He would, however, have been willing to lead the campaign.

But knowing the policies of the different powers and their jealousies of one another, he was forced to reconcile himself to the idea that there was little chance of his being able to induce the nations to co-operate under his leadership as his father had done. His political schemes — which fitted in with those of Europe as a whole — required a basis of facts, not of mere expectations, if they were to be successful. Thereupon he set about establishing himself so firmly in the political life of western Europe that his would be last word in the shaping of international events. He knew he could count on the support of the Papal See, which as one of the temporal powers in Italy was dangerously threatened — politically as well as spiritually — by the incursions of the Crescent. But the Pope's support, though important, was not sufficient in itself: the Christian masses of the west were indispensible to his plan.

The lessons of history had shown Matthias that the only way to rouse the nations was through the German Emperor. If only he could be made to take the initiative and accept the leadership! But Frederick III, the acknow-

MATHIAS REX MANU PROPRIA
KING MATTHIAS' SIGNATURE

ledged temporal head of Christendom, was concerned solely with his ambition to increase the territorial might of his own dynasty, and did not seem to possess either the qualities or the inclination for embarking on such a bold enterprise. On the contrary, it was almost certain that even if it meant running counter to the desires and convictions of the rest of Europe, he would more likely frustrate than promote the scheme. These considerations led Matthias to conceive the idea — which later was to shape his whole policy — of acquiring the Imperial crown himself and so realize his plan of European co-operation.

This was the sole aim of his ambition. A man free from vanity, he looked upon the Imperial throne merely as an instrument for the furtherance of his anti-Turkish policy, which, we repeat, was in accordance with the vital interests of the Christian nations. The long wars with Bohemia, which exhausted Hungary's military and financial resources, were all undertaken with this object. The acquisition of the Bohemian crown would, he hoped, establish immediate association with the German Empire, for the King of Bohemia was one of the most important German Electors. As King of Hungary and Bohemia he hoped to make a bid with some prospect of success for the crown of the Holy Roman Empire as soon as it required a successor. Unexpected opposition in Bohemia and the duplicity of Frederick frustrated his plans. Nevertheless, he annexed the greater part of Bohemia and Silesia, and in the course of his wars with the Emperor occupied Lower Austria and Vienna. The control of these territories fostered the hope that his campaign against the Turks might yet be realized, but death overtaking him at the age of fifty (1490) put a sudden end to his activities.

The Bohemian and Austrian wars had forged Hungary into a first-rate military power. Following implicitly the example of his father, Matthias abandoned the obsolete method of raising troops by calling upon the nobility. He maintained instead a standing army of volunteers, later to be known as the "Black Host," which was composed of infantry and artillery. He personally supervised the organization and training of his forces, which came to be regarded as a model army, Youths from other countries were eager to go to Hungary to learn the art of war. The outstanding feature of this army was its discipline, which was highly praised by foreign visitors who had the opportunity of visiting the King's headquarters when manœuvres were in progress. His staff was excellent, and with its assistance his campaigns were highly successful. This was due not so much to the size of his army as to its skilful handling. One of his most brilliant exploits was the defence of Breslau. In 1474 Matthias with an army of about 10,000 soldiers was garrisoned in Breslau, the capital of Silesia. The Poles and Bohemians attacked the city with forces six times the strength of the Hungarian garrison. Nevertheless, thanks to the King's strategy, it was the enemy that sued for peace and ultimately accepted very hard terms.

This exhausting warfare and the upkeep of a standing army laid very heavy financial burdens upon the country. In order that it should be able to bear them Matthias made strenuous efforts to promote the economic prosperity of the population and increase their tax-paying capacity, and he did much to alleviate the lot of the serfs. The fact that his army consisted mainly of foreign mercenaries left the Hungarian population free to increase even in times of war. During his reign the valley of the Middle-Danube was a highly prosperous and well protected region, well-deserving to be called the bulwark of Christianity by the rest of Europe. A spirit of national consciousness pervaded all classes, and everyone looked up to the King as the most just and disinterested protector of his subjects' interests. The King made no discrimination between them, but rewarded or punished each according to his deserts. Birth was powerless to shield the guilty, nor was high station or rank allowed to be an excuse for evil-doing. The petty affairs of the humblest of his serfs were not considered too mean for his personal attention, and when it seemed expedient, he pronounced judgment in person. His judges, imbued with the same spirit, dealt justice to the meanest of his subjects, even as they did against the most powerful of the feudal lords. This uncompromising impartiality has preserved his memory green in the hearts of the Hungarian people.

The observer will notice something Roman-like in the figure of the King in Fadrusz's work. We are to some extent reminded of the Roman Emperors, as portrayed in ancient sculpture. In presenting Matthias thus Fadrusz wished to point to the intimate relationship between the King and the civilization of ancient Greece and Rome. At the time of the Renaissance, when the masterpieces of those ancient civilizations began to be again studied and cultivated, King Matthias Corvinus held a very high position among the European monarchs as a Mæcenas of science and art. He set an example in the Royal palaces in Buda, Visegrád, Tata, and Vajda-Hunyad that was followed in the episcopal residences and the castles of the aristocracy, which became centres of learning and the arts. Foreign — chiefly Italian and German — scientists, the so-called Humanists, poets and artists flocked in great numbers to Hungary, while Hungarian scholars, bards and artists were welcome guests at the Courts and other centres of learning in western Europe. Legends were in circulation concerning the pomp of Matthias' Court, about his learning and erudition and his famous library of manuscripts. Some of these even now rank among the most precious specimens of their kind. His name is bound up with the foundation of the universities at Buda and Pozsony (Presburg) and with the creation of the first Hungarian scientific society, the members of which were the most eminent scholars of their age. King Matthias reorganized

STATUE OF KING MATTHIAS
John Fadrusz

Kolozsvár (Transylvania)

STEPHEN BÁTHORY, PRINCE OF TRANSYLVANIA AND
KING OF POLAND

From a contemporary portrait
Ambras Collection, Vienna

education and, by sending hundreds of youths to foreign universities he forged cultural and literary links with western Europe. In his reign Hungary became an important member of the civilized Christian world, and her King one of the leaders of European intellectual and political life.

WLADISLAS II AND LOUIS II.

(1490—1516, 1516—1526)

Matthias and John Corvinus. Election of Wladislas II. The personality of the new King. The Diet of 1505 on the plain of Rákos. Family links with the Habsburgs. Dózsa. The peasant rising under Dózsa. Struggle for power between the nobility and gentry. Turkish aggression in 1521. Decline of prosperity. The defeat at Mohács.

In the midst of carrying his schemes King Matthias suddenly fell ill and died in Vienna, a city much favoured by him during the latter years of his life. His death meant not only the ruin of his plans, but also the beginning of new trouble. Like many of our kings, Matthias left no heir fit to continue his work and proceed with his far-seeing policy, for his adopted son John Corvinus was a man lacking determination. Nevertheless the King had come to regard him as his heir and during the last years of his reign had done everything to secure his succession. He had endowed John Corvinus with vast estates and great power and at the Diet of Vác 1485, he had had the functions of the Palatine increased and this high office conferred on his uncle Emery Szapolyai, in order to assure as far as possible the succession of his adopted son. The Holy Crown was committed to his care and the most powerful lords both spiritual and temporal were bound by oath to support his election. After his death, however, these precautionary measures proved abortive.

Matthias had ruled with an iron hand, brooking no opposition even from the most powerful nobles who had long been accustomed to regard themselves free from all interference. True, attempts to resist him had been made, but without success and the King had even imprisoned his uncle Michael Szilágyi and his former tutor John Vitéz, Archbishop of Esztergom, for their refusal to obey him. The nobles felt oppressed as by a nightmare by the powerful personality of Matthias and breathed more freely when they heard of his death. Several of them, indeed, let it be plainly known that they would now elect a king whom they could firmly control.

Opposed to those nobles who were only concerned for their own personal interests were others who above all things were determined that Matthias' policy should be continued. They argued that though Matthias had ceased fighting the Turks, it was only because he considered Hungary too weak to pit herself against the Turkish Empire. It had been to increase the resources of his own country that he had tried to conquer Bohemia, Moravia and Silesia, and hence they now advocated the election of Wladislas of Bohemia, asserting that he would be able to carry out Matthias' great schemes without any undue sacrifices being called for. Wladislas was supported by Matthias' Italian Queen, Beatrice, because he might become what John Corvinus never could, *i. e.* her future husband. Wladislas was finally elected, many voting for him because they desired a weak and irresolute king, such a one as by common report they had reason to believe Wladislas was likely to be.

John Corvinus, whose chances of election had originally seemed rosy enough was finally left without supporters. He was deserted by all. Even after the election, wishing to retire with his troups beyond the Drave, he was attacked by the partisans of Wladislas under that same Paul Kinizsi who was famous for his victory over the Turks at Kenyérmező, and who owed his splendid military career to King Matthias. At this encounter which took place near Sárviz, John Corvinus was defeated and compelled to surrender to Wladislas.

By the election of Wladislas II (1490—1516) Bohemia, Moravia, and Silesia were united with Hungary under one crown. So far, the object of those who claimed that the election of this King would best promote the schemes of Matthias, had been attained. But it soon also became obvious that those who had voted for him merely because they wanted a weak king had found a man entirely after their heart. Wladislas was certainly a good and well-meaning man, but at the same time one who had the greatest difficulty in refusing anything to anybody. According to tradition, his favourite expression was a Polish word — he was a Pole of the Jagello house — meaning "All right" and in Hungarian history this epithet has remained associated with his name, and to this day he is commonly referred to as Wladislas Dobjy. Thus, in a very short space of time everything in Hungary that could possibly be given away was given away and every thing that could be granted, granted. Finally even the royal estates fell into the hands of strangers, and the resources necessary for the up-keep not only of the Royal Court, but even of the public services, vanished. Science and art, on which King Matthias had spent so much, languished and finally became non-existent for lack of support. The royal funds were squandered, and the rarest books in the world-famous library of Matthias fell into the hands of foreigners. No money remained even for the defence of the country. The Black Army of Matthias went unpaid for a long period, and the soldiers were driven to violence and outrage. This redoubtable force was eventually disbanded by its commander, Paul Kinizsi, in 1492. Even the frontier garrisons lacked supplies and ammunition, and but few years after the death of Matthias Hungary presented a sad spectacle of desolation and decay. She was without money and men.

This state of affairs, in which the country was being sacrificed for the benefit of certain individuals, brought about a strong reaction. The more the patriotic Hungarians saw of Wladislas, the more unfavourable was the comparision with Matthias, and the deeper grew their disappointment and discontent. The gentry became more and more convinced that the fount and origin of all their troubles was the King, who knew neither the language nor the laws of the country and was thus a pliant tool in the hands of the nobles and prelates. Thus it happened that at the Diet of 1505, held on the plain of Rákos, it was declared and enacted that in future because in the past the kings of foreign origin had been the chief cause and authors of "the terrible dismemberment and shocking decline of the country," of the loss of its provinces and frontier fortresses, and because the kings of Hungarian stock had, on the contrary, "worked for the welfare and expansion of the kingdom," upon the death of King Wladislas, should he leave no natural heir, no foreigner should be elected king "but only a Hungarian fit and able to discharge the duties of royalty."

This enactment, ruthlessly criticizing and even stigmatizing as it did the rule of Wladislas, was something unprecedented in the history of Hungary. It marked a serious decline in the royal authority and showed the deep gulf dividing the gentry, who formed the effective majority of the nation and were already organized as a political party, from the King. Wladislas realized that he had lost the confidence of the majority of the people and was dependent on the aristocracy alone. This support he felt to be insufficient, for well he knew the antagonism dividing the various sections of the greater nobles from one another. He was concerned not so much for the future of the country as for that of his children, Anne and Louis. Distrustful of the Hungarians, he was obliged to seek an alliance with a strong foreign dynasty and turned to the Habsburgs. The Emperor Maximilian gladly received his overtures, hoping thus to acquire a certain family lien on Hungary and Bohemia. Negotiations spread over several years and eventually resulted in the engagement of Wladislas' son, Louis, to Mary, the Emperor's granddaughter, and of the Emperor's grandson, Ferdinand, to Anne, the Hungarian King's daughter. At the same time a mutual agreement concerning the right of succession was also arrived at by the two monarchs.

In this way Wladislas gained what he wanted: the future of his children was, or seemed to be assured and other things scarcely mattered. Yet the peasant rising of 1514, if nothing else, might have warned him that he was building on sand.

The lot of the peasantry had grown rapidly worse under Wladislas. What with church tithes, landowners ninths and other imposts and taxes, it had never been

POZSONY IN THE XVI CENTURY

From a contemporary engraving

an easy one, but under Matthias they had at least the protection of the law which that King had upheld even against the most powerful. Moreover, he had never concealed his opinion of the value of the peasant as a national asset. Many tales were current among the peasantry about King Matthias, his justice and his sympathy for themselves. There was, for instance, the story of Matthias and the nobles he had set to dig in his garden. They had soon grown exhausted from this physical work, and the King took the opportunity of pointing the moral, that having learned by experience how arduous was the act of digging, they should thenceforth appreciate the labour of those who had to pass their whole lives engaged in such work Another story concerns Matthias and the Sheriff of Kolozsvár. The latter abused his authority to compel the humble folk to saw and chop wood for him without payment. By chance, on one occasion, when Matthias happened to be staying in Kolozsvár in disguise, the Sheriff pitched on him and ordered him to split wood in the public square. The King meekly set about the work, but cut his name on every log he split. When he subsequently made a state entry into the city, and the Sheriff appeared before him to answer the King's questions and assure him that he was carrying on the King's business according to the law, Matthias sent for the logs with his name carved on them as proof that the Sheriff had misused his powers, and had him severely punished.

"But Matthias is dead, and justice has died with him" — so ran the proverb and so it runs even to this day. Under the feeble hand of Wladislas, the peasantry were without protection against the rapacity of the landowners. As their grievances increased, so did their sullen resentment when with full knowledge of the conditions no one in authority did anything to help them. Such was the state of affairs when Thomas Bakócz, Archbishop of Esztergom, with the approval of the Pope and the Hungarian Parliament started to preach a crusade against the Turks. Everyone was called upon to rally beneath the banner of the Cross. The peasants responded with enthusiasm, and assembled in great numbers in the crusaders' camp near Pest. In some places the landlords, who viewed with anything but favourable eyes the departure of their workers at the time when the land needed them most, tried to restrain them from going by force. When reports of deeds of violence reached the camp, the crusaders' wrath was roused and soon it was openly declared that the landlords were even greater enemies of the people than the Turks and should be dealt with first. This was also the opinion of George Dózsa a gentleman by birth and the commander of the crusaders. Under his leadership the revolt spread like wildfire throughout the country.

The onslaught of the peasantry came with such suddenness that their opponents were given no opportunity to organize effective resistance, and had it not been for the timely intervention of John Szapolyai, the Voivode of Transylvania, the whole country would have fallen into their hands. Even so, the rebellion wrought great havoc and loss on the country.

Once defeated, the peasantry were entirely at the mercy of their conquerors. The Diet of 1514 was consumed by a spirit of unbridled revenge. The peasants were penalized with fresh burdens and denied the right to choose their place of abode. The result of these measures was to create a bitter feud between the two largest classes of the nation — the peasants and the squires — at the very time when more then ever before a united front was imperative. It was to the throne of a distressed and divided country that Louis succeeded on the death of his father in 1516.

Louis was not yet of age and it had been the wish of Wladislas that he should be placed under the joint guardianship of the Archbishop of Esztergom, John Bornemissza, the Captain of Buda, and the Margrave George of Brandenburg his kinsman. But the Diet decided otherwise. It declared Louis to be of age and appointed him a council of sixteen to assist him with the administration of the State. Nothing was done as regard his education, which was held to be a private matter for the royal family to arrange, who raised no objection when the three nominees of Wladislas offered to take over the education of the young King. The boy was intelligent and serious-minded, fond of sport and conscientious in his duty. He might have developed into a fine man and able monarch had he not fallen completely under the influence of his kinsman, the Margrave George. George was a frivolous person who displayed considerable originality in the pursuit of his pleasures, and obtained such an ascendancy over the young King that he was able entirely to debauch his character.

With a boy King, the country fell a prey to faction. The nobles and gentry pursued their own interests to the total disregard of the welfare of the country as a whole. A decrease in public revenues, frivolous prodigality at Court (owing to which the frontier fortresses lacked supplies and fell into disrepair), the army unpaid, decline of trade, debasement of the currency — all these evils passed unheeded in an orgy of selfish lust for power. No one was concerned about the relations of Hungary

with foreign countries, or whether any outside help
would be forthcoming should the country be attacked.
Even the Turks were totally forgotten. Fighting,
indeed, was continuous on the frontier, but there

SOLIMAN II
From a contemporary engraving

was a formal truce, frequently renewed, that lulled men into a false sense of security. All the greater was the surprise, therefore, when it became known that the new Turkish Sultan, Suliman II, irritated because his envoys had been in error thrown into prison in Buda, had declared war and was advancing with an army on the Danube. In 1521 he attacked and captured all the fortresses on the southern frontier. Belgrade, Sabatch, Zimony, Szalánkemény and Titel were lost, and the road into Hungary lay open. A rebellion in Persia, however, distracted the Sultan's attention, and thus for a time at least the threat to Hungary abated.

But the loss of these strongholds caused great consternation throughout the country. Party strife ceased in the face of the common danger. Laws, decrees and resolutions were passed to consolidate the national power. Then came the news that events in Persia had put an end to the Turkish invasion, and with the removal of the immediate pressure, faction lifted its head once more.

Foreign observers saw in Hungary a country drifting headlong to disaster. The Papal Envoy, Baron Burgio, held Louis responsible in the first place for the deplorable state of affairs. He reported him as lacking in every kingly virtue. Serious matters he found tedious, he avoided the meetings of the Royal Council whenever possible, and even when present he jested with members throughout the sitting. The duties of government were attended to by the Margrave George, whose main interest was dancing. After the marriage of the King in 1521, things went from bad to worse. Queen Maria shared her husband's tastes. At Court entertainment followed entertainment. The result of all this was that the royal authority was so completely ignored that finally anyone might enter the palace at will and sit at the King's table. But this was not all. The frivolity of the Court, it is true, offended the more serious minded, but since a similar state of affairs was not uncommon elsewhere at the time it might have been borne with resignation. The Court, however, was not alone frivolous, but was also German — and that was intolerable. According to the Papal Envoy, the King's only interest lay in German affairs, and he and his entourage thereby completely alienated the sympathy of the Hungarians. Even the nobles and bishops, who had at first supported the Court, came to share the universal hatred. The gentry, who were numerous and claimed to represent public interest, aspired to greater power, and demanded as a pledge thereof, the right to appoint the Palatine. These claims were resisted by the nobility and a bitter party struggle ensued. In 1525 the squires' party succeeded in deposing the leader of the nobles, Stephan Báthory, from the Palatine's office, and secured the election of Stephen Verbőczy, the eminent jurist and author of the celebrated code, "*Opus Tripartitum*," whose statue now stands in Apponyi Square in Budapest. But though the men differed, the system remained the same. A little later we find the Papal Envoy reporting that every man pleased himself, that there was no longer any authority, no jurisdiction, and no prospect of their being re-established. Factions strove for political power solely in order to promote private interests. All this at a time when at any hour might come news of a Turkish invasion. Self-sacrificing patriotism alone might have averted disaster, but as the Pope's Envoy wrote, if the price of Hungary's escape from the sore straits in which she found herself had been three florins, three men would not have been found to pay them.

The new Palatine was unable to effect any improvement in the hopeless condition of the country. He was more or less a tool in the hands of the different parties, and had been but a few months in office when the squires who

Tripartitum opus iuris consuetudinarij inclyti regni Hungarie: per magistrū Stephanum de Werbewcz personalis presentie regie maiestatis locum tenentem: acuratissime editum.

THE FIRST LINES OF STEPHEN WERBŐCZY'S "TRIPARTITUM"
(1514)

had elected him withdrew their support in disappointment, with the result that he resigned in 1526 and retired to Transylvania. Stephen Báthory then returned to office and the extreme conservatives to power. Their aim was to maintain the *status quo* and nothing could have been more fatal in the circumstances. It was common knowledge that the Sultan Suliman II, was hastening his preparations for invasion. Paul Tomori, the wise and heroic Archbishop of Kalocsa who was in command of the southern forces, repeatedly sent warnings and appeals for help, but in vain. For months his soldiers were without pay, and

a wretchedly equipped, starving army and crumbling fortresses made resistance hopeless. Again to quote the Papal
Envoy: "Your Holiness must be prepared to find this
country quite unable to defend itself and entirely at the
mercy of the enemy. How can Hungary be expected to
wage war with unpaid soldiers on the frontiers? The King
is so poor that he cannot even supply his own table. The
nobles quarrel among themselves and the squires are
divided into conflicting parties. But even were they
united, what could they do against the Turks, lacking as
they do, the means of warfare? They might fight one
battle, and face certain defeat. I do not understand much
about war, but if the Turks seriously attack this country,
I see no possibility of saving it."

In the history of every nation vacillation and lack of
will power are the surest signs of decay. During the six
months before the battle of Mohács, they were much in
evidence in Hungary. The Sultan began his advance at
the end of April, 1526, when it was too late to do anything.
When King Louis set out from Buda on the 20th July to
meet him, the army under him consisted, in all, of three
thousand men.

The Turkish forces under the command of the Sultan
himself amounted to 80,000 men and from 160 to 200
guns. By the end of August the Hungarians mustered
25,000 men and 85 guns. But the Turks were superior
not alone in numbers, but also in discipline and training.
Besides, the Hungarians lacked a commander-in-chief.
Paul Tomori, the valiant soldier-priest invited by the King
at the last moment to take command, declined on the
ground of his lack of strategical knowledge. Finally the
command was divided between John Szapolyai, Voivode

of Transylvania, and his younger brother, George. There was no man, however, who had the will to lead. The Voivode counselled withdrawal to await reinforcements, but the temper of the army compelled the commanders to

PORTRAIT OF LOUIS II
From a contemporary engraving

offer battle on ill-chosen ground near Mohács. Here, on August 29th 1526, a great disaster, in which half the army, its two commanders, the Archbishop of Esztergom, several bishops and numberless nobles perished, overcame unhappy Hungary.

133

Louis whose conduct during the weeks preceding the battle had been exemplary, distinguished himself in the fight. After the rout he tried to make the Buda road, but became bogged in the mud of the brook Csele, which had been swollen by heavy rains, and weighed down by his heavy armour he perished miserably, the place being marked today by a memorial column. His death atoned somewhat for the many errors of his life. After the battle the Hungarian dead were buried by one Dorothea Kanizsay, whose name will remain immortal.

CARDINAL MARTINUZZI (FRIAR GEORGE).
(† 1551)

Struggle for the Hungarian throne between John Szapolyai and Ferdinand I. Interference of the Turks. Loss of Buda. The constitution of the Transylvanian Principality. Life of Friar George. Part played by him in support of John Szapolyai and his son, John Sigismund. Attempts to restore the integrity of the country. Death of Friar George and its consequences.

The battle of Mohács marked the beginning of a new epoch in the history of Hungary. The old rivalry between the two parties continued to be as acute as ever. One party rallied round John Szapolyai, the Transylvanian Voivode, the other round the Court. Party strife continued as if the defeat at Mohács was of no more consequence than other similar misfortunes in the history of the country, from which the country had gradually recovered. The burning question of the day was that of the succession to the throne.

The opposition, which had long contended for a real national life in Hungary, thought that its hour had arrived and rallied round John Szapolyai. It was composed mainly of squires, who attributed all their misfortunes to the foreign kings and were ready to believe that a king of Hungarian stock would put everything right. The Court and nobility thought otherwise. They had plans to offset the defeat at Mohács by a foreign alliance. They attributed the disaster to the isolation of the country and held that its evil consequences might be averted with the help of some strong western European power. Everything point-

CARDINAL MARTINUZZI,
FRIAR GEORGE'S SIGNATURE

ed to the Habsburg Empire as the power in question. This division of opinion was the country's misfortune. Each party held obstinately to its own point of view. They hated each other, even after Mohács, more than they loved Hungary, and rather than renounce party ends they allowed the country to fall a prey to the Turks.

The Voivode was not the man to grasp the situation, to discover the right line of policy to be adopted. His one and only solution for all the problems involved was to fill the throne in accordance with his own personal ambitions. But hardly had he been elected (Nov. 5, 1526) when he realised that his authority was not to pass unchallenged. The Court party chose a rival king, Ferdinand of Habsburg and brother of the Emperor Charles V (Dec. 16th 1526). They hoped by this to secure the moral and material sudport of the Empire. The result of this double election was civil war.

Fortune at first favoured Ferdinand. Early in 1527 King John was forced to flee to Poland, whence he planned to reconquer his kingdom. This period marked a change in his policy. He changed from a vacillating to a determined man and was guided by clearly formed ideas towards well-defined objectives. This was brought about by a simple Pauline friar, Utyesenitch alias George Martinuzzi, commonly known as Friar George.

He was of Croatian extraction but had lived from his early youth in Hungary and was a good Hungarian. In his youth he had been in the service of King John's mother, the Duchess of Teschen, — it is said that as a boy he tended the stoves — and thus became acquainted with the most trusted supporters of the Szapolyai family. Later he joined the Pauline Order and his brilliant qualities soon brought him into prominence. In his flight to Poland King John stopped to rest in the monastery of Sajólád near Miskolc and found his Abbot to be none other than the former family retainer. In the course of conversation it soon transpired that the friar's robe concealed a statesman. It was evident that Friar George knew much more about the temper of the country, the strength of the parties and their leaders than the King himself. King John therefore took Friar George with him to Poland as his Privy Councillor.

After Mohács Friar George was the only Hungarian statesman who strove with singleness of purpose for the restoration of Hungarian territorial integrity and the cessation of party strife. He aimed at the creation of a united Hungary firmly ruled by a national king. In the struggle to attain this he was constantly obliged to change his tactics and methods, to suppress his private feelings, and to suffer bitter disappointments, and finally he was forced to admit that he had failed.

His fate was tragic. He was the only Hungarian statesman of the time to realize Hungary's international situation. He understood that, isolated, Hungary could not exist. She had to be brought into the sphere of interest of one or other of the great European powers. He knew that the Turkish Sultan was already in alliance with Francis I of France, the deadly foe of Charles V and the Habsburgs. Under these conditions he considered King John's chances of ruling as an independent king to be hopeless. He was dependent on foreign support and the only place to find this was in the anti-Habsburg camp. This led to the idea of a Turco-Hungarian alliance, a thing hitherto unheard of. John Szapolyai and the Sultan came to terms and in 1529 and 1532 the latter led his army in person against Vienna, in order to crush the power of the Habsburgs in eastern Europe. These campaigns were unsuccessful and as a result the majority of the towns of Hungary were left little more than smoking ruins. Friar George realised that the Turks had failed him. King John's party, indeed, came to be hated and scorned by the patriots as the Turkish party. So he turned to the Habsburgs with the idea of effecting a compromise whereby it was to be understood that the two Kings were to be recognized in the territories held by them respectively, but on the death of John, who had no children, the whole country was to be united under King Ferdinand and his heirs.

This was the substance of the Peace of Nagyvárad 1538.
Ferdinand, however, did not trust John and nothing came
of this peace. King John died in 1540 and Ferdinand tried
to win his territory by the sword. This brought the Sultan
into action once more. In 1541 Suliman entered Hungary
at the head of a large army to support the claims of John
Sigismund, the son that had meanwhile been born to John
Szapolyai. The fortress of Buda fell into the Sultan's
hands and with it a great part of the Hungarian Alföld

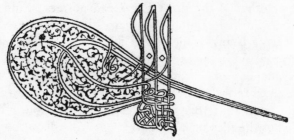

SOLIMAN II'S SIGN-MANUAL
From a photograph

(Lowlands). By the express wish of the Sultan, John
Sigismund with his mother, Queen Isabel, and Friar
George retired to Transylvania. The country was now
divided into three parts. Friar George was in a difficult
position. Either he had to give up the policy of unity
hitherto pursued and acquiesce in a tripartite division of the
country, or find some other way of realising his original
aim. He chose the second alternative. The Sultan, he
knew, would never agree to give up any part of the territory
he had conquered; thus Martinuzzi was driven into the
arms of the Habsburgs. But he had not forgotten the

lessons of the past. Overdue haste was to be avoided lest the autonomy of Transylvania, which had meanwhile been made an independent principality, be endangered. Thus while he negotiated with Ferdinand and even formally handed over Transylvania to him (Gyalu — 1541), he also kept in touch with the Sublime Porte, paid a regular annual tribute, and repeatedly sent envoys to Constantinople to secure the Padisha's support for Transylvania and John Sigismund.

The purpose of this double-faced policy was to avoid the danger of a Turkish war until the Habsburgs were strong enough to attack the Turks with success. He had no intention of jeopardising what remained of Hungary for the sake of private interest, dynastic or otherwise. Vienna, naturally, was not very enthusiastic about his policy. Neither Ferdinand nor his generals trusted him. They regarded him as the real enemy of Hungarian unity. When Castaldo, Ferdinand's general in Transylvania, reported that Friar George was hand in glove with the Turks, and suggested that matters would be simplified by putting him out of the way, Ferdinand raised no objection to the suggestion. So Castaldo had the Cardinal — for he had attained this dignity — assassinated on the 17th December 1551, in his castle at Alvinc. Thus perished the only man of statesmanlike qualities who might have been able to bring about the restoration of Hungarian unity. The fatal consequences of this crime were soon apparent. Sultan Suliman made it a pretext for further aggression against Hungary. In 1552 he laid siege to such fortresses as had hitherto held out against him. Temesvár fell after a heroic defence under its commander, Stephen Losonczy, Drégely fell and George Szondy with it, Szolnok was basely surrendered by its garrison of foreign mercenaries, and other smaller strongholds in the north fell into the Sultan's hands. Only the fortress of Eger, defended by Stephen Dobó, held out. There the garrison fought with such heroism that the Turks were at last compelled to raise the siege.

Ferdinand was not able to hold Transylvania, which he thought had fallen into his hands after Martinuzzi's assassination. The people soon came to hate the new administration with its arbitrary methods and heavy taxes. John Sigismund, who had received two small Silesian Duchies as compensation for the loss of Transylvania, and Queen Isabel were far from satisfied with their circumstances and wishful to return. At the express desire of the Sultan, they were reinstated and took over the government of Transylvania in 1556, so that this country was again separated from Hungary.

STEPHEN BOCSKAY, PRINCE OF HUNGARY AND TRANSYLVANIA.

(† 1606)

The Transylvanian Principality. Extension of Turkish Rule. Prince Sigismund of Transylvania and King Rudolph allied against the Turks. Decline and decay of Transylvania. Life of Stephen Bocskay. His military exploits. The Peace of Vienna. Death of Bocskay.

Ever since St. Stephen's time Transylvania had been a part of Hungary. Under the Árpáds and their successors it had been a Voivodate ruled by a Voivode appointed by the Hungarian King. After Mohács the eastern part of the country was made a separate state, a principality, first under John Szapolyai and John Sigismund and later under the Báthorys. For more than a century Transylvania realized the idea of an independent Hungarian state.

The Hungarians were united in their resentment of the partition of their country and the domination of the Turks. Turkish rule meant desolation and the practical enslavement of the population. The regions of Alföld and Trans-Danubia to the east of lake Balaton became depopulated. The sites of many once prosperous towns and villages are today indicated by mounds and ridges which still bear the old names. The Turks subsequently enlarged their conquests still further when after 1591 Nagykanizsa, Eger, and several other places fell to them. Only a narrow strip on the frontier was left to the Habsburgs. The rest was in the hands of the Turks who had but one political creed: to root out all infidels.

In Transylvania Sigismund Báthory was Prince. He was cousin to the Stephen Báthory who succeeded John Sigismund, and he was elected King of Poland in 1576, to become one of Poland's greatest kings. Sigismund Báthory hated the Turks and tried desperately to get rid of them. Many others, however, held the view that Turkish suzerainty, however objectionable, at least meant the preservation of peace in Transylvania and permitted the development of that country. If the ן rincipality — it was argued — broke with the Turks and rallied to the side of Hungary, it would provoke the Turks to vengeance and Transylvania would be turned into a battlefield on which all the fruits of years of peace would be lost. Such prudent considerations, however,

HUNGARIAN HUSSAR IN THE XVI CENTURY

From a contemporary woodcut

made less impression upon the Prince than the illusions fostered in him by foreign emissaries, whereby he was led to see himself as a hero of Christendom, a great captain heading a European alliance which would deliver Europe from the Turkish yoke and set Hungary free.

These romantic dreams made it difficult for him to listen with patience to the advice of the so-called Turkish Party and he finally sent their leading representatives to the scaffold in 1594, and forced the Transylvanian Estates to accept an alliance with Rudolph, King of Hungary, against the Turks. This new turn in the policy of Transylvania was mainly due to one of Sigismund Báthory's kinsmen and councillors, Stephen Bocskay. Bocskay came of an old Hungarian family, and his father, who was brother-in-law to Dobó, the hero to Eger, had held a position at Court. Much of Stephen Bocskay's childhood had been spent in Prague and Vienna under Court influences. As a court page, he had been carefully educated, and later he was admitted into the company of aristocratic pages who were personal attendants of the King and the Royal Family. This was a much coveted distinction sought not only by Hungarian families but also by those in other European countries, and it left an indelible impression on him. He saw the riches and splendour of a Court which was a centre of politics, science and art. He was fascinated and dazzled and thought that the power of the Habsburgs was irresistible. The thought of the contrasting misery and poverty in his own country, led him to believe that its only hope of salvation lay in alliance with that great Empire whose ruler was also the legitimate wearer of St. Stephen's crown.

On his return home he went to live at the Court, since he was closely related to the Prince's family. There he soon became the leader of the so-called "German Party" and was largely instrumental in bringing about the change in Transylvanian policy already mentioned.

The first result of this Germanophile policy was war with Turkey, in which Báthory was at first successful. It was not long, however, before the joint forces of Transylvania and the Empire were defeated at Mezőkeresztes, whereupon he abdicated and after prolonged negotiations handed over Transylvania to Rudolf.

His abdication was the beginning of one of the saddest periods in the history of Transylvania. The country was garrisoned by hostile foreign mercenaries who robbed and harassed the population. Very soon Sigismund Báthory began to regret his abdication, and between 1598 and 1601 he returned three times to Transylvania and was thrice elected Prince, without, however, being able to re-establish the former independence of the country against Rudolph and his generals. The principality, so lately a flourishing country became the scene of incessant wars and in a few short years fell into utter ruin. Plague and famine added their horrors to the desolation of war, and not infrequently (especially among the Walachian population) instances of cannibalism are recorded. The advisers of Stephen Báthory were held responsible for this desperate state of affairs, and were promptly exiled. Among them was Stephen Bocskay.

This unfortunate man retired to his estate in the county of Bihar. There he learned that conditions in Imperial Hungary were no better than they were in

Transylvania. The country was in the hands of plundering soldiery. Nobody was safe, even the most powerful nobles were in danger of being arrested on trumped-up charges and seeing their estates confiscated. No protection against these outrages was afforded by the two independent Courts, the Palatine and the Diet.

It is characteristic of the situation that Bocskay, whose pro-Habsburg policy had brought about his expulsion from Transylvania, was eventually driven to take arms against the Imperial generals, whom with the assistance of the Haiducks he defeated in 1604. Thereupon the Estates of Hungary and Transylvania elected him Prince. The Sublime Porte supported him, even sending him a crown, so that the Austrian Court, residing at the time in Prague, was willy-nilly obliged to negotiate with him, though only for a short time, before branding him a rebel. The Peace of Vienna in 1606 brought redress for all former grievances, re-established the Palatinate and the legislative power of the Diet, proclaimed religious freedom and acknowledged the independence of Transylvania. This last condition was particularly stressed by Bocskay who considered it the surest guarantee that Hungarian national sentiment and ideals would be safeguarded. Through this peace tranquility was restored and Hungary secured to the Habsburgs.

The other great achievement of Bocskay was a treaty concluded with the Turks in 1606, which put an end to continuous warfare, and secured peace to Hungary for a time.

But Bocskay himself was not permitted to direct the work of reconstruction the foundation of which he had laid, for he died quite suddenly in December 1606. The Peace of Vienna was undoubtedly the basis of a new Hungary. The subsequent struggles were in fact carried on to defend the constitutional privileges secured by that treaty.

GABRIEL BETHLEN, PRINCE OF TRANSYLVANIA.

(1613—1629)

Bocskay's successor in the Transylvanian Principality. Gabriel Báthory. Gabriel Bethlen and the Viennese Court. His wars in defence of the Hungarian constitution. Result and importance of his rule.

Bocskay's time was too short to enable him to make good all the losses sustained by Transylvania in the troubled years and especially during the times of the Voivodes, Basta and Michael. It needed many years of wise and careful government to restore Transylvania to the position she had occupied when Sigismund Báthory began to reign.

Bocskay's immediate successor was Sigismund Rákóczi, an old man not in full possession of his faculties, who abdicated within a year. Gabriel Báthory who followed him, was, on the contrary, too young and inexperienced for the position, and was, besides, irritable and extravagant and brooded no contradiction. Under his rule violent religious and national conflicts arose in Transylvania. He made enemies of the Catholics, who conspired against him, and oppressed the Saxons, who refused to obey him. When the general feeling had turned against him he tried to find support in Vienna, and was quite ready to sacrifice Transylvanian independence to obtain it. Matthias II (1608—1619), who succeeded Rudolph, received his overtures gladly. They came to an agreement which, however, availed nothing against the national movement led by Gabriel Bethlen and backed by the Turks. Gabriel Báthory was finally compelled to flee and on his flight met with death at the hands of the Haiducks.

His successor was Gabriel Bethlen, a man who from early youth had participated in the political life of his country, and had soon revealed qualities of greatness. This had been recognized, and during the troubles that followed the abdication of Sigismund Báthory the Transylvanian emigrants offered him the ducal coronet. Bethlen, however, declined the honour and remained loyal to Bocskay and his successors until driven to rebellion by the misconduct of Gabriel Báthory. His election as Prince was viewed with consternation in Vienna. It was felt that the much desired incorporation of Transylvania in the Empire was now farther off than ever. The Vienna Court had always distrusted Bethlen, refused to acknowledge him as Prince, and schemed to deprive him of the support of the Sublime Porte, even to turn it against him. These Viennese intrigues created much trouble in Transylvania. The Saxons in 1614 were incited to counter-revolution and the Haiducks and Siculians were encouraged to secede. Vienna in fact was ready to support anything and anybody against Bethlen. It was therefore natural that the latter took the opportunity offered by the Bohemian rebellion of 1618 to ally himself with the Bohemians against the Emperor.

At that time Hungary was in a turmoil of discontent with the Imperial rule. All the grievances that had formerly driven the Hungarians into Bocskay's camp

GABRIEL BETHLEN, PRINCE OF TRANSYLVANIA
From a contemporary engraving

were once again the cause of complaint. Accordingly, when Bethlen advanced westward, he met no opposition till he came to Pozsony. Feeling that the Hungarian constitution was at stake, great numbers flocked to his standard. The Estates even elected him King of Hungary. But Bethlen was wary and when he learned that the Emperor was willing to enter into negotiations on the basis of the Peace of Vienna and at the same time give him the pledges of good faith he desired, he agreed to come to terms and peace was signed in 1622 at Nikolsburg in Moravia between him and Ferdinand II. By this peace he attained his ends. Transylvania added considerably to its territory and the Emperor promised to respect the Hungarian constitution as defined in the Peace of Vienna.

The terms of this agreement, however, were not observed by the Court of Vienna, and Bethlen on two further occasions took the field against Ferdinand, each time as the ally of England, France, Holland, and Denmarks. As a result, the Treaty of Nikolsburg was renewed.

Transylvania's role in the wider sphere of European polities increased the prestige both of the little State and of its Prince, especially when he married Catherine of Brandenburg and thus became the brother-in-law of Gustavus Adolphus, King of Sweden. A section of the Poles would gladly have seen him King of Poland. But Bethlen had other plans. He had become convinced that the Turks were a broken reed, and he aimed at restoring the integrity of Hungary by means of a great European alliance which would be strong enough to drive them out. But his schemes were suddenly brought to an end by his unexpected death in 1629, when he was barely 49 years old.

The golden age of Transylvania is bound up with his name. When he took over the country in 1613, it was improvised and torn by faction and little more than a tool used ruthlessly by both sides in the long-standing feud between the Empire and the Turks. He was successful in putting an end to internal dissension and in uniting all classes in support of what was really for the good of the country as a whole. Toward the nationalities his policy was wise and conciliatory. He tried to reconcile Saxon and Hungarian, and to raise the standard of life among the Wallachians. Those of that race, for instance, who distinguished themselves in the service of their country were raised to the rank of Hungarian nobles, according to ancient Hungarian custom. He wished to have the Bible translated into Wallachian, and even hoped that they might be converted to Calvinism.

Bethlen was a fervent Calvinist and an eager student of Holy Writ. At the same time he held the religious opinions of all in respect, even when they differed from his own. Of his two chancellors, one, Simon Péchy, was a Sabbatarian, or Seventh-Day Baptist, while the other, Stephen Kovacsóczy, was a Catholic. Another of his friends was the Jesuit George Káldi, to whom he rendered assistance in publishing his translation of the Bible, and who was more than once employed by him in political matters. Even Jews and Anabaptists received privileges in the interests of trade. In an age of intolerance, such broad-mindedness was almost unique.

Besides questions of Church and State, he gave serious attention to culture and education. As early as 1614 he had a law passed that schools were to be founded all over the country. Another law provided special protection for the clergy, teachers, and students. The Diet of Kolozsvár, 1615, ordained that two-thirds of the money accruing from fines imposed for transgression of church regulations should be spent by the cities and boroughs on churches and school building. In 1624 it was further enacted that free schooling was to be provided for the children of serfs, and landlords found guilty of preventing their serfs sending their children to school were fined one thousand florins. Under the wise guidance of Gabriel Bethlen it came to be accepted in Transylvania that since scholars and scientists were of great value to the state, systematic provision for their education was an important duty of the nation.

Bethlen was a nationalist, but an enlightened one, who realized that national character might be enriched by intellectual contact with other countries. He therefore favoured and sought to promote closer contact with the West. Students were encouraged to study at foreign universities, were even supported while there, and only those who had an acquaintance with the higher branches of learning were admitted to the civil service. It was almost unique how this man with a burden of public cares that few could have shouldered found time to keep in personal touch with his protegees and remain informed of the progress they made in their studies.

His principal foundation was the famous college of Gyulafehérvár, which remained for centuries the focus of western culture in the east of Europe.

Among the subsequent professors of the Gyulafehérvár college mention must be made of Isaac Basire who fled from Durham in England when the rebellion against Charles I broke out. He was professor of the Gyulafehérvár college from 1655 to 1661 and played an important rôle there.

Gyulafehérvár was a place of which Bethlen was very fond. There he made a prince's capital out of what before had been but a small town. He was much given to building; besides his palace at Gyulafehérvár, he reconstructed the great castle of Vajdahunyad. Transylvania in his day recalled the times of Matthias in Hungary, when art and learning flourished as never before. The Prince's recreation after the struggles of the battlefield and the council chamber, was to engage in theological and political discussions with scholars, listening to Italian music, or viewing the dramatic performances given regularly at his Court. He resolved to raise every Reformed minister to noble rank, in order to ensure that the ministry would always command the services of the best in the land. It may also be of interest to note that in the XVII and the beginning of the XVIII century it was the custom for Transylvanian students of Calvinist theology to spend some time at English universities. We know the names of 135 or 140 of students who did so. That this custom of "peregrination" was commented on in England is seen from the following quotation from Milton: "Nor is it for nothing that the grave and frugal Transylvania sends out yearly from as far as the mountainous borders of Russia, and beyond the Hercynian wilderness, not their youth, but their staid men, to learn our language and our theologic art." (Areopagitica.)

All these in themselves were acts that deserved to endear the memory of Gabriel Bethlen to his countrymen. They were all the more remarkable in that he considered himself to be and was, first and foremost a soldier. He had been brought up practically in camp, where there was little opportunity of acquiring learning. But there were always books among his baggage, so that by reading he might supply the deficiency left by lack of regular schooling.

But not only was he a great and successful soldier, against whom even the great Wallenstein was chary of risking his prestige in battle, and a generous patron of learning, he was also a great statesman. Nothing proved that more conclusively than when he refused to accept the Hungarian crown, preferring rather the substantial advantage of enlarging the frontiers of his own principality and so make it of some account in European politics. Under him Transylvania became something to reckon with, not only in Vienna and Constantinople, but also in London, Paris and Stockholm, and her Prince would even have been welcomed as King of Poland. Gabriel Bethlen, indeed, was a great creative genius who saved his country from its decline and set it on the highroad to the fulfilment of its destiny in the history of Hungary.

CARDINAL PETER PÁZMÁNY.
(† 1637)

The Reformation. Its growth in Hungary. Importance of Protestantism. The Society of Jesus and its activity. Peter Pázmány's career. Pázmány and the Turkish question. Pázmány and Transylvania. His endowment of schools.

Just twenty-five years after the discovery of America, an obscure Augustinian friar nailed a document containing 95 theological theses on the door of the church in Wittenberg. (October 31th 1517.) By this act Martin Luther

PROPOSITIONES THEOLOGICÆ
AVSPICIIS
Eminentissimi Principis
PETRI· CARDIN· PAZMANY
ARCHIP· STRIGONIENSIS·PRIMAT·
HVNG·S SEDA LEGATI NATI·z̄c.
defensæ
a Georgio Pohroncio Szelepchenij Vng.
Coll:Ger: et Vng:Alum⁹

entered the arena of European politics and the Reformation was formally inaugurated.

The movement reached Hungary actually through the townsfolk of German origin, but the doctrines of the Reformation were also much canvassed at the Court of Louis II which was largely German. Owing to the anti-German feeling prevailing among the squirearchy a prejudice against the teachings of the Reformation prevailed in the more distinctively Magyar circles of the nation where they were regarded with suspicion, as being the thin end of the

PETER PÁZMÁNY'S SIGNATURE

German wedge. In 1523—1525 enactments were passed by the Estates enjoining that severe punishment be inflicted on proselytes. After Mohács, however, with the entire country in confusion, there was no question of enforcing these enactments, and both Luther's and Calvin's teachings spread rapidly. Generally speaking, people of Slav and German origin preferred Lutheranism, whereas the majority of Hungarians became Calvinists. Calvinism, indeed, came to be known as "the Hungarian religion."

The national character of the Reformation helped to explain its rapid development. The vernacular was used

155

alike for worship, preaching and the reading of Scripture. Copies of the Bible translated into the common speech were disseminated by thousands and schools were built so that the people might be taught to read them. On the other hand, the chance of obtaining church lands easily and other less worthy motives also played their part, so that in the course of a generation after Mohács most of the Hungarian people belonged to one or other of the Reformed Churches.

Then came the Counter-Reformation. The Jesuit Order was founded in 1540 and became at once the spearhead of renascent Catholicism. The Jesuits adopted the Reformer's methods, and the energy and skill they brought to their task soon produced considerable results. They came to Hungary in 1561, and Nicholas Olah, Archbishop of Esztergom, who was closely related to the Hunyadis, built a school for them. At the invitation of the Báthorys they entered Transylvania in 1580, where a school-building and a printing office were placed at their disposal by the Prince.

The Jesuit college in Kolozsvár soon became famous and was attended by the children of the nobility, even of the noble Protestant families. One of the students was Peter, son of Nicholas Pázmány, Vice-Lieutenant of the County of Bihar. Under the influence of the school he turned Catholic in 1583 and later entered the Society of Jesus. On finishing his studies he became a teacher of the High School in Graz, Styria. While there, he followed with interest the controversy raging in books and pamphlets between the two religious parties, and even took part in it himself. His writings and his sermons delivered in racy Hungarian soon made the Catholics look upon him as their natural leader. In 1616 he was appointed Primate of Hungary, and used the great power and prestige conferred upon him by this exalted office so skilfully that to a great extent he was able to attain the aims of the Counter-Revolution.

Pázmány was convinced that the Turks, who occupied the largest and by far the richest part of Hungary, constituted the greatest danger to his country. To be rid of them, it was necessary to face them with a firmly united front. All obstacles to unity had to be removed. Most important of these in his eyes were the antagonisms and dissensions provoked by religious differences. His missionary zeal was directed not only towards defeating the Reformers but also to producing a solid united Hungary.

But he was also well aware of the danger threatening from the Germans on the eastern marches. Writing to Gabriel Bethlen in 1626, he says: "It seems to me that we are squeezed between two powerful Empires like a finger between folding doors." He favoured, therefore, united action on the part of the Hungarians, who were at that time divided into eastern and western *blocs*, and did not wish them to waste energy and resources in useless warfare. He opposed Bethlen's belligerent policy, and writing on one occasion to George Rákóczi I, Prince of Transylvania, he said: "I should like to have this little stock of Hungarians spared for better times and to prevent them destroying one another. Providence may one day have mercy upon us and save us from our natural foe the Turk." His anxiety for the future of the Hungarians led Pázmány to oppose the Court and then the Palatine, Nicholas Eszterházy, and he became champion and protector of Transylvania. Transylvanian separatism was in his eyes one of the bulwarks of Hungarian freedom against the encroachments of the Court of Vienna. He once said that the Hungarians had prestige and credit at the Imperial Court only so long as Transylvania existed. "When she ceases to exist," he added, "the Austrian will promptly spit upon us." In accordance with these views he supported Gabriel Bethlen's successor, George Rákóczi (1630—1648), in opposition to the Palatine, Eszterházy, and he continued to favour him till his death, though Rákóczi was an ardent Calvinist.

As a Cardinal he was also a conscientious churchman. He tried to raise the material and spiritual standards of the clergy. When he took over his diocese it could hardly count a hundred priests, and many of these were intellectually and morally far from what they should have been. To remedy matters he founded a college for Hungarian priests, the Pazmaneum, in Vienna, which exists at the present time. He founded another seminary at Nagyszombat and by means of large endowments made it possible for the more gifted among the priests to continue their studies in Rome in a special foundation for Hungarians created by one of the Popes.

The education of the laity was also his care. At that time the Catholics were badly provided with schools, whereas the liberality of the Prostestants had led to the establishment of a number of excellent and flourishing colleges. In Gabriel Bethlen's schools rich legacies had made higher education accessible even to those of humble means. Pázmány's schools and colleges in Nagyszombat were founded with a similar end in view. Poor students had the opportunity of receiving an excellent education

BUDA AND PEST IN THE XVI CENTURY

From a contemporary engraving

there, and nothing was asked of them in return but loyalty to their country. For the purpose of higher academic learning he founded a college in Pozsony which he handed over to the Jesuits, of whom in general he was an ardent supporter.

His greatest foundation was what is now the University of Budapest. Founded in 1635 at Nagyszombat it originally consisted of two faculties, theology and philosophy. Later law and medicine were added. In 1777 Maria Theresa transferred it to Buda and gave it accomodation in the Royal Castle. In 1783 it was removed to Pest. It is the oldest and largest university in the country.

No one felt more strongly than Pázmány that rank and dignity had duties as well as privileges. He was a loyal and liberal supporter of the causes of the Church, the nation, and learning. Even his opponents recognized his nobility and generosity of mind and character. Bethlen himself and all his Protestant contemporaries esteemed him as one of the greatest men of his time. He died in 1637 mourned by all Hungarians, Catholics and Protestants alike. With him, it was felt, one of the strongest pillars of the Hungarian national cause had ceased to exist.

COUNT NICHOLAS ZRINYI, SOLDIER AND POET.

(† 1664)

Suliman II's campaign. Szigetvár. Nicholas Zrinyi's self-sacrifice. The Zrinyis and the Turks. Nicholas Zrinyi's youth. Literary work. Building of the Zrinyi-ujvár castle. Winter campaign of 1664. Battle of St. Gotthard and Peace of Vasvár. Death of Nicholas Zrinyi.

In 1566 the old Sultan Suliman crossed the Hungarian frontier for the seventh time in his life. In the interests of his protegee John Sigismund, Prince of Transylvania, he prepared to attack Maximilian, the German Emperor (and King of Hungary 1564—1573). The immediate object of his campaign was to conquer Szigetvár, the biggest fortress in the counties to the south of Lake Balaton. The commander of this castle, Count Nicholas Zrinyi, was much hated and feared by the Turks as one of their strongest opponents. After unsuccessful threats and negotiations the Sultan gave orders for the attack on Szigetvár.

For the garrison the choice lay between surrender and death, and they determined to resist. Attack after attack was repulsed with a valour that aroused the admiration even of the Sultan himself. He offered Zrinyi new terms of surrender, but Zrinyi, though he saw his cause was hopeless, refused to discuss surrender. Suliman thereupon offered a reward of a thousand florins to any member of the garrison who brought him Zrinyi's head. No traitor, however, was to be found among them. The intensity of the fighting increased until the castle

NICHOLAS ZRINYI, THE HERO OF SZIGETVÁR (†1566)

From a contemporary engraving

became a ruin. Then Zrinyi, in his robes of state, distributed money among his men, and headed a last desperate sortie. After a violent struggle he fell together with most of his followers. The Grand Vizier sent his head to the King of Hungary, who was at that time idly encamped with his army near Győr. A young English nobleman who was to become famous later on also took part in the defence of Szigetvár. This was Sir Richard Grenville of whose daring adventures on

SIGNATURE OF NICOLAS ZRINYI,
SOLDIER AND POET

the "Revenge" extraordinary tales were in circulation in contemporary England.

Zrinyi's name and fame were blazoned all over Europe. The defence of Szigetvár was celebrated both in prose and verse, and its valiant commander was hailed as one of the heroes of Christendom.

The traditions of the family were worthily upheld by the great-grandson of the hero, who was not only a soldier, but also a poet. He wrote the first epic poem in Hungarian, and chose for his theme the exploits of his great ancestor. The poem was entitled "The Peril of Sziget."

The poet Zrinyi was left an orphan early in life and was brought up by his guardian, Peter Pázmány.

11*

All the circumstances of his life, therefore, combined to imbue him with a hatred of the Tuks and strengthened a resolve to do all in his power to rid Hungary of them.

In Pázmány's house he had excellent opportunities of equipping himself for the duties and responsibilities of public life. In Vienna great things were hoped of Zrinyi and his brother. They were expected in time to prove useful instruments of the ruling dynasty. While yet quite a child, young Zrinyi was appointed Grand Master of the Horse, Chief Lieutenant of several counties and Captain of Muraköz. As a stripling he became a general and the Ban of Croatia. Everyone expected that he would be the future Palatine, and he soon became one of the most popular men in the country.

Zrinyi himself was ambitious to secure the post in order to have larger scope for his energies. But the Court was not pleased with the manner in which he was identifying himself with the Hungarian cause, and opposed his election. The neglect of the frontier fortresses by the Viennese authorities thereby leaving the heart of Hungary exposed to the attacks of the Turks, aroused Zrinyi's indignation and called forth energetic protests from him. Seeing the defences crumbling and the garrisons without food and munitions, he even came to suspect that there was more design than mere neglect in the treatment meted out to Hungary.

At this time misfortune overtook Transylvania. The ambitions of Prince George Rákóczi had entangled the little principality in wars which had given the Turks the chance to attack her, and she had lost a considerable amount of land to the Sultan. Yet even thus weakened she appeared to Zrinyi to be the main Hungarian base for an attempt to drive the Turks out of Hungary. He was all in favour of the Hungarians relying solely on themselves in this undertaking. Foreign aid he considered a broken reed and also too expensive. He therefore advised that Hungary should maintain a standing army ready for immediate action whenever the need arose.

Many at that time considered the Hungarians unable to deal with the Turks. Zrinyi was well aware of the disparity in numbers and resources, but he was convinced that there was enough vigour and valour in the Hungarian people to prove the sceptics wrong. Accordingly, without asking money from Vienna, he built a new castle on the Mura called Zrinyi-újvár, and made it the centre of active aggression against the Turks in the neighbourhood.

The activities of the Zrinyi brothers created considerable uneasiness among the Turks, and the Grand Vizier ordered the Pasha of Nagykanizsa to be strangled for allowing Zrinyi-újvár to be built, and also sent repeated messages to Vienna protesting against the action of the Zrinyis and threatening war if nothing was done to stop them.

The Vienna Government might have been willing to purchase peace at that price, but the arrogance of the war party among the Turks was such as to make war inevitable sooner or later, so that even the most accomodating of Vienna Governments could not avoid the outbreak of hostilities that began in 1663.

The Zrinyis now had the chance for which they were both fully prepared. Peter remained in Zrinyi-újvár, while Nicholas joined the Imperial forces on the Vág. There he found no inclination to come to blows with the enemy. When the Turks stormed Érsekújvár, no attempt was made to relieve it. On his own initiative, however, Zrinyi succeeded in bringing off one brilliant exploit against the Turks, when he saved the island of Csallóköz in the Danube and released some thousands of Christian prisoners. This achievement proved his quality as a strategist and a leader of men.

He soon returned to Zrinyi-újvár and from thence, while the Imperial Council in Vienna deliberated about money and supplies, he took the offensive, annihilated several hordes of Turks, captured the important bridgehead at Eszék, and so prevented the Turks from crossing the Drave. This he achieved in bitter winter weather and with small forces.

All Europe rang with his fame. The Pope and the King of France sent him letters of congratulation and German towns arranged thanksgiving processions in his honour. But the Imperial Court showed but scant enthusiasm and when the Turkish army renewed its attack upon Zrinyi-újvár, the Imperial commander refused to give the brothers any assistance. Zrinyi-újvár fell and the hordes of Osman would have overrun the whole district of Muraköz but for the titanic efforts of the two Zrinyis.

After the fall of Zrinyi-újvár the Imperial army gained a victory over the Turks at St. Gotthard (August 1664). But the fruits of this victory were entirely thrown away by the conclusion of the shameful peace in which the Turks gained all they might have won by a successful battle.

COUNT NICHOLAS ZRINYI, POET AND SOLDIER

From a contemporary engraving

The peace exasperated the whole nation, and it was openly said that the country had been betrayed. The feeling was widespread that something had to be done. The Palatine, Francis Wesselényi, and the Primate, George Lippay, Archbishop of Esztergom, joined Nicholas Zrinyi in a movement which is generally known as the Wesselényi Conspiracy.

But in November 1664 Nicholas Zrinyi's career was brought to a sudden end. He was out shooting with a young Transylvanian nobleman, his guest at Csáktornya, and on his return in the evening one of his gamekeepers reported that he had wounded a wild boar without killing it. On hearing this Zrinyi at once returned to the wood, leaving his guests to wait for him. Suddenly a man ran up to them with the news that something serious had befallen their host. When they found him he was dead. The old boar's tusks had gored him so savagely that he bled to death almost immediately.

When the news of his death spread people were incredulous. It was widely believed that he had been assassinated, and though his companion, Nicholas Bethlen, vouched for the genuinness of the tragedy the conviction of foul play remained in the public mind for centuries.

FRANCIS RÁKÓCZI II, PRINCE OF HUNGARY AND TRANSYLVANIA.

(† 1735)

Wesselényi's plot. "Kuruc" and "Labanc." The Hung-arian constitution abolished. Emery Thököly's insurrection. Wars for liberty. The Parliament of 1687. The Kolonics system. General discontent. The Rákóczis. Youth of Francis Rákóczi II. Struggle for liberty. Peace of Szatmár. Rodosto.

The indignation and unrest aroused in Hungary by the Peace of Vasvár did not subside even after the death of the great national leaders, Nicholas Zrinyi, the Palatine Francis Wesselényi and George Lippay, Archbishop of Esztergom. Others rose to take their places and head the national resistance against the policy of the Vienna Government which was growing more and more un-bearable. These new leaders were Peter Zrinyi, Ban of Croatia, Francis Nádasdy, Chief Justice, and Francis Frangepan, who were later joined by Francis Rákóczi I, Peter Zrinyi's son-in-law and Prince-elect of Transylvania. After long deliberations they resolved to break away from Vienna and create an independent Hungary with French or Turkish help. The Imperial Government, however, had an intricate system of informers and the conspiracy was stifled in embrio, the leaders being executed (1671), with the exception of Francis Rákóczi who was pardoned on payment of a large ransom.

Though Vienna knew that this conspiracy was but the attempt of a few individuals for which the nation could not be made responsible, Hungary was nevertheless reduced in status to a province like the so-called hereditary lands of the Habsburg family. Leopold I (1657—1705), a weak Emperor completely under the influence of his councillors, was prone to believe that the movement had been mainly Protestant and was induced to order the persecution of the Protestants. School and churches were confiscated and the landed gentry of all denominations burdened with crushing taxation, to enforce the payment of which the country was garrisoned with hostile foreign troops, — from whom there was no security of person or property — who had, of course, to be paid and fed by the population. Thousands fled to Transylvania and the Turkish provinces where they rallied into bands and carried on guerrilla warfare against the Imperial troops and on all suspected of serving the Vienna Government. Some initial successes emboldened these homeless refugees to embark upon greater enterprises, but they were completely crushed in 1672.

The Imperial Government took this success to mean a smashing victory over Hungary, and considered that the country's power of resistance had at last been broken. Vienna proceeded to abolish the constitution and Hungary was definitely declared an Imperial province. A German governor was appointed over the country and everybody held to be sympathetic to or harbour relations with the wandering bands of fugitives was put through a cruel inquisition. The Protestants were regarded as a political party and an attempt was made to exterminate them. In Pozsony an extraordinary tribunal tried several hundred Protestant ministers and teachers and sent them to the galleys. The people were divided into two parties, the "*Kuruc*" and the "*Labanc,*" (similar to the Roundhead

HUNGARIAN HUSSAR AND HEYDUCK

From a XVII century engraving

and Cavalier parties in England), each bitterly hostile to the other, and the strength of the country was heavily drained by this internecine strife.

The fugitives kept up their guerrilla warfare for years, but without any signal success. Prince Michael Apafi of Transylvania showed them both sympathy and good-will, which did not help them much. (In England the Whigs displayed so much sympathy with Thököly's politics that the members of that Party were called "Teckelists" by the Tories and in contemporary English literature. Several of the satirical poems about the "Teckelists" are still in existence. Pamphlets and historical works of that period treat of the hero of Hungarian Independence whose name was as well-known in England as those of Bethlen, Zrinyi and, later, Rákóczi.) It was only when Emery Thököly became their leader that their cause assumed national importance. He disciplined them and with their aid conquered Upper Hungary, where he was elected Prince. Then at length the Vienna Government was forced to see that the policy of arbitrary despotism had failed and that, if the Emperor was to keep any hold on the country at all, it was imperative to revert to constitutional methods. The Diet of Sopron (1681), therefore, re-established the constitution, elected a Palatine, and promised to redress all political and religious grievances.

This satisfied the bulk of the nation, and when Thököly expressed dissatisfaction and continued his struggle, he was abandoned by most of the people. There were rumours of another Turkish war, and it seemed criminal to weaken the national front by civil strife in face of the Turks. When the Turkish advance

172

began Tököly's position became untenable, for though he was a political ally of the Turks, the anti-Turkish feeling of the nation compelled him to remain inactive and when the news came that the Turks had been repulsed before Vienna, his *Kurucz* force dispersed in all direction (1683). The success at Vienna inspirited the Imperial authorities and they elaborated a great plan of attack against the Turkish power in Hungary, hoping to destroy it and liberate Hungary from the yoke it had borne for 150 years. Thus by the irony of fate, the Imperial forces set themselves to realize what had been the dream of every Hungarian for more than a century. Thököly's troops joined them in the campaign, and on 2nd September, 1686, the Imperial army, whose cosmopolitan ranks included several thousand Hungarians who distinguished themselves in this battle, took Buda by storm.

The fall of Buda undermined the *morale* of the Turks. Fortress after fortress fell into the hands of the Imperial forces. Belgrade was taken in 1688 and an advance made into the Balkans. After the battles of Szalánkemény (1691) and Zenta (1697), nothing remained of the Turkish Empire in Hungary except Temesvár and the country round it.

The integrity of Hungary was restored after a century and a half. The Emperor ruled over a united country as its King, even Transylvania acknowledging his supremacy. Leopold was not slow to exploit the prestige that the successes of his troops had won for him. At the Diet of 1687 he demanded that Hungary should forego the right to elect its own king and should instead, recognise the hereditary right of the male line of the Habsburg family. Secondly, that the clause of the

EMERY THÖKÖLY, PRINCE OF HUNGARY

From a contemporary engraving

Golden Bull which empowered the nation to take arms against unconstitutional rule, should be rescinded. Both these demands were acceded to by the Diet.

In the general atmosphere of joy following the expulsion of the Turks it would have been very easy for the Government to wipe out the memory of old wrongs completely. All that was necessary was tact and consideration. The Hungarians were willing to be loyal subjects of their Habsburg king, so willing that they even let Emery Thököly die in exile in Turkey. But the rulers at Vienna neither liked nor trusted the Hungarians. The foreign mercenaries ruled the people with a reign of terror. In Eperjes General Caraffa arrested, imprisoned and put to death the leading citizens of the town on mere suspicion. Crushing taxes and religious persecution soon made people realize that they had been better off under the Turks. In Vienna no secret was made of the intention to introduce a new system of government in Hungary, and the constitution was repeatedly and openly violated. All this awoke a storm of indignation, the danger of which was obvious to everyone except the powerful ones in Vienna. When Francis Rákóczi headed the great national movement the Imperial Court was completely taken by surprise.

In the Rákóczi family reverence for the Hungarian constitution was a traditional sentiment. One of Francis' ancestors, Sigismund had been a follower of Bocskay and subsequently his successor as Prince of Transylvania (1606—1608). George Rákóczi I, Prince of Transylvania who concluded the Peace of Linz (1645) which guaranteed political and religious liberty to Hungary was his great grandfather, and George Rákóczi II,

Prince of Transylvania, who had the laws of the principality codified, was his grandfather.

His father narrowly escaped with his life for his share in Wesselény's plot. Of such ancestry was the man who was predestined to champion the cause of his downtrodden country in evil times.

Francis Rákóczi II was born on March 27th 1676 at Borsi in the Country of Zemplén. His father died the same year and his education was in the hands of his mother, Ilona Zrinyi, Peter Zrinyi's daughter. She was actively concerned in Thököly's rebellion and married him in 1682. When his fortunes were on the wane, for three years she heroically held the last of his strongholds, Munkács, against the Imperial troops. Finally when the town was forced to surrender she and her daughter were taken to Vienna, and her son sent to a Jesuit school in Bohemia to be educated as a good Imperialist, where he passed several years and at which he was not even allowed to speak Hungarian.

When he came of age, he married and returned to his ancestral estates. There he was under the continuous surveillance of spies employed by the Vienna Government. Austria had reason to fear him, for he was desperate at the dreadful condition of Hungary, and felt so acutely for his people that when he thought the time ripe he risked all in one desperate throw for his country's freedom.

The game was all but lost before it had scarcely begun through the treachery of a man whom Rákóczi had always considered a particularly faithful friend. It so happened that France, looking round for some means of causing the Emperor embarrassment, had her attention directed to the deplorable state of Hungary and

176

the feeling against the Government prevailing there. A correspondence sprung up between Rákóczi and the French, in the course of which Rákóczi was promised French support, were he to revolt against the Emperor. The intermediary in these negotiations was a Captain Longueval, an intimate friend of Rákóczi. This man, however, was at the same time an agent of the Imperial Court who callously betrayed the trusting Rákóczi. The latter was arrested in April, 1701, and imprisoned in Wiener-Neustadt. At his trial his false friend represented the prosecution, and there is no doubt that Rákóczi would have suffered the same fate as his uncle, Peter Zrinyi, — from the very same cell — at the scaffold, had not his wife bribed the governor of the castle to connive at his escape. He soon managed to reach Poland, where he joined his friend Count Nicholas Bercsényi who had also been compelled to flee for safety in consequence of Longueval's treachery. Rákóczi used the time spent there in securing the assistance of the French for Hungary, and got into touch with disaffected Hungarians. In Hungary everything was prepared for his coming. The peasantry in particular was eager to welcome him and in the meantime harassed the *Labances* and Imperial garrisons. That in itself did not much embarrass the authorities and the peasant bands were soon dispersed, but this did not in the least discourage Rákóczi from entering Hungary to put himself at the head of the national cause. He was coolly received, however, by the nobles and gentry, who thought he relied too much on peasant support, and called him "the peasants' leader." But when they found that he was no mere class leader, but determined to lead a united country, they flocked to his standard, for their lot under the Imperial regime was as hard as that of the peasantry. In the course of the year 1703 the whole country, except

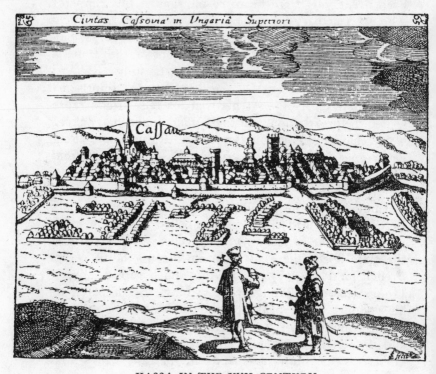

KASSA IN THE XVII CENTURY

From a contemporary engraving

Trans-Danubia, rallied round him. *Kuruc* flying columns ventured into Austria and Moravia, and even appeared in the neighbourhood of Vienna to the consternation of the citizens.

178

Leopold was preoccupied with his war against France and in no condition to deal energetically with Rákóczi. He was accordingly only too ready to treat with him and make him lavish promises. But Rákóczi was too astute to trust in words only. He wanted solid pledges. He insisted that Transylvania should be independent and under his rule, and that its independence must be guaranted by foreign powers, especially by Holland and England. To this the Emperor would not agree, neither would Rákóczi yield, and negotiations were broken off.

The struggle continued with changing fortune. Rákóczi was elected Prince of Transylvania in 1704, and Prince of Hungary in the following year and governed with wisdom and moderation. Religious troubles were eliminated and by a series of well-timed measures he hoped to restore economic prosperity. But economic conditions were desperate, and in spite of all he could do, it did not seem possible that they could be improved. The promised French subsidies did not arrive, public revenue had fallen off and the gold and silver gone to provide munitions of war. Disaffection began to show its head among the masses. The situation was so serious that Alexander Károlyi, commanding the *Kurucz* forces entered into negotiations with the other side on his own responsibility, as a result of which the Peace of Szatmár was concluded (1711).

By this treaty the constitution of Hungary was recognized but not the independence of Transylvania. Rákóczi took it as a sign of defeat, and though his personal safety and possessions were assured, he preferred to go into exile rather than acquiesce in a state of affairs he believed and had always proclaimed to be unsound.

He died at Rodosto on the Sea of Marmora in 1735, much to the relief of the Imperial authorities who had kept a anxious eye on him till the end. His name has always been held in reverence throughout Hungary, as one of the noblest figures in her history, and in 1906 his remains were brought home from Constantinople and interred with solemn national ceremony in the ancient Cathedral of Kassa.

QUEEN MARIA THERESA.

(1740—1780)

Charles III and the Pragmatic Sanction. Accession of Maria Theresa. War of Succession and the Seven Years' War. Public education in Hungary. The aristocracy in Vienna. The Life Guards. Economics. The problem of the serfs. Customs Policy.

When the Diet of Pozsony relinquished its right to elect the king and settled the succession on the male heirs of the Habsburgs, the matter seemed to be closed. But it so happened that at this time there was a most unusual scarcity of male heirs in the Habsburg family, for neither Joseph I nor Charles III had left sons behind them.

Charles was well aware of the serious consequences that would ensue should he die before the law of succession was modified in order to secure the throne to the Habsburgs. He knew that the loose conglomeration of races

PORTRAIT OF FRANCIS RÁKÓCZI II

From a painting by Adam Mányoki, XVIII century
Original in the Museum of Fine Arts, Budapest

STATUE OF MARIA THERESA
John Fadrusz
Pozsony (Czechoslovakia), demolished in 1921

and nations that made up his Empire might easily fall
into disintegration were the succession disputed. He
therefore took steps to alter the constitution and secure
the throne to the female line also. It was no easy matter
to persuade the Estates to agree. Nevertheless fortune
favoured him. Under Eugene of Savoy his troops were
victorious in a campaign against the Turks, in which
the last vestiges of Ottoman power in Hungary were
destroyed. Temesvár was recaptured and the ancient
frontiers of Hungary completely restored. The great
national rejoicing which resulted from this made it
easier for the King to induce the Estates to accept the
Pragmatic Sanction which embodied the new law of
succession (1722—1723).

On the death of Charles III his daughter, Maria
Theresa (1740—1780), ascended the throne of St.
Stephen. Her constitutional title was recognized
throughout Hungary, but there were still others to
question it. There was indeed an undignified scramble
for the Habsburg possessions on the part of numerous
claimants, and Frenchmen, Spaniards, Bavarians, and
Prussians marched into the Empire to take what they
could get. All seemed lost for poor Maria Theresa.
But she was a woman of spirit and in her distress she
appealed to the traditional chivalry of the Hungarians.
She approached the Estates sitting in Diet at Pozsony
in 1741, wept before them, and won the whole assembly
to her side.

Nor was the vote mere lip-service. The country
was with her to a man, and a large and well-disciplined
army was placed at her disposal. The fortune of war
turned and before long she had won back all that had

been lost except Silesia, which was in the firm grip of Frederick the Great. The war ended in all parties recognizing the validity of the Pragmatic Sanction. Hungary also loyally supported the Queen in the Seven Years' War which followed.

Maria Theresa was not unmindful of the services of the Hungarians. She longed to give peace and prosperity to the country and to see a contented population of faithful subjects living in peace and friendship together. She saw clearly that reforms were necessary. Unfortunately the nobility and gentry had not the same breadth of vision. As a class they had ceased to take the same active interest in public affairs as their fathers. Most of them lived on their estates, cultivating their land, and their outlook was sadly limited. New ideas in the matter of scientific government were entirely unknown to them. But even had this not been the case it is not likely that they would have felt inclined to support them. Preoccupied as usual with their own petty interests, their attitude towards public affairs was dominated by a rooted disinclination to change anything.

Maria Theresa had many opportunities of studying this obstinate conservatism. At the Diets she heard, on the one side, a long tale of grievances and met, on the other, an obstinate resistance to any suggestion of a modification of the old order i. e. of the privileges of the nobility. At length she grew impatient of diets and preferred to carry her reforms by decrees.

These fall into two categories, cultural and economic. Before Maria Theresa's time education was in the hands of the denominations and cities. No other bodies had the right to found and manage schools. The utmost the State did was to control the Protestant schools whenever the Protestants were considered an untrustworthy element in the State. When, in 1772, the Pope dissolved the Order of the Jesuits, Maria Theresa saw that the time had arrived for the State to take a more active and prominent part in public education. She ordered curriculums for primary and secondary schools to be drawn up, which were later made compulsory for all schools, and entrusted the supervision of school administration to school inspectors and district headmasters.

She built schools by law in various towns, enlarged the University of Nagyszombat by adding a medical faculty, and transferred the whole institution to Buda.

The Queen's object was not only to raise Hungary to the level of contemporary civilization, but also to narrow the gulf which separated Hungary from the western states. To further this she had the teaching of German made compulsory in all secondary schools. A boarding-school, moreover, for the sons of the nobility was founded in Vienna, in which a large number of the scholarships were reserved for Hungarians. Here, it was hoped, the Hungarian nobility would acquire a taste for the learning and refinement of the West. This Theresianum, as it is called, exists under altered conditions at the present day. But Maria Theresa did not rely upon education alone to strengthen the links binding Hungary to her capital. New social bonds were formed, designed to attach the Hungarians to her Court. She kept open house in Vienna where the nobility from all the provinces of her Empire were made welcome, and it soon became the fashion for the Hungarian nobles to go to Vienna. There they learned Viennese manners, the German, French and Italian languages, and developed a taste for western art and literature. The Queen was markedly gracious to those members of the nobility who fell in with her ideas. She founded the orders of Maria Theresa and St. Stephen, and was generous in the matter of conferring decorations, dignities and offices. In this way a more intimate relationship was established between the different aristocracies of the Empire. Later, some of the Hungarian nobles acquired permanent residences in Vienna and lived there most of the time. Indeed it happened that quite a number of Hungarian nobles forgot their own language, forgot even that they were Hungarians.

The smaller squires, living their rural lives in the country, remained indiffernt to Vienna. If one or other of them had reason to visit the capital, he was all the time ill at ease and glad to get back home again. The Queen's method of dealing with the squires was original and ingenious. She formed a regiment of Hungarian Life Guards Her intention was to recruit this regiment from among the younger members of the gentry who would be nominated by the different counties from time to time, and she hoped that during their period of service they would develop an affection for Vienna and its culture which would remain with them as a permanent civilizing influence when they returned to their respective homes. To a certain extent her expectations were fulfilled. The young men were impressed by Vienna and admired what they saw there, but they proceeded to draw conclusions unforeseen by the Queen. The intellectual life of Vienna awoke in them a desire to revive intellectual life in Hungary and to use the Hungarian language, which had fallen into disuse, in place of Latin which was then generally spoken in the higher social circles. Their ambition was to encourage the gentry to read, and as a means to this end they set themselves to the task of developing and refining the Hungarian tongue. The quarters of the Hungarian Life Guards in Vienna were actually a school where grown men were to be seen at their studies, prompted by the ambition to teach later on and to show the world that Hungary was as grateful a soil for the seeds of science, literature and art as any in Europe. It was from among these young Life Guards that the pioneers of a renascent Hungarian literature arose.

From the outset Maria Theresa was aware that the economic problems calling for solution were formidable. The burden of taxation had been greatly increased not only by the protracted wars but also by an expanding administration and the new splendour of the Court, and the Queen was obliged to find fresh sources of public revenue. To her credit she understood that the only sound way of doing this was to develop commerce and industry upon which taxes might be levied. The question of taxation drew Maria Theresa's attention to the condition of the serfs. The Estates with their provincial outlook and narrow conservatism were strongly opposed to any reform in this direction. The Queen, however, overcame their opposition and issued an ordinance not only granting the serfs the right to settle anywhere in the country but also permitting their children to be educated for any profession they might choose. Furthermore she fixed the maximum the serfs could be asked to pay in taxes and other services. The burden on the serfs continued to be heavy enough, but they were able to invoke definite legal protection against the tyranny of their masters. This was a very important step forward in the social life of Hungary.

Public works of all kinds — drainage schemes, road-making, the harnessing of water power, etc. — were initiated to increase agricultural production. The Government devoted special attention to mining, forestry, and cattle-rearing, and Maria Theresa secured the port of Fiume for Hungary to give Hungarian trade free access to the sea.

There was wisdom in this economic policy, but the results of the various enterprises and reforms were not immediately forth-coming, and the Government was in immediate need of money. The Estates were definitely opposed to further taxation and the Queen shrank from encroaching formally on the right of the Diet to vote supplies. However, she found ways of raising money not provided for in the constitution. Previously all the Habsburg dominions formed a customs union, and were protected against foreign competition by a high tariff wall. Maria Theresa introduced a new customs policy based on the idea that it was Hungary's business mainly to produce and supply the raw materials needed for manufacturing purposes by Austria, Moravia, and the other hereditary provinces of the Habsburgs. She set up a customs barrier between Hungary and the other countries of the Empire with the result that the hereditary provinces obtained their raw materials cheap from Hungary, for, the market being restricted by law, there was no competitive buying. The hereditary provinces, allowed, as they were, to monopolize the Hungarian market and manipulate prices, grew rich at Hungary's expense, and the Government, taking its toll of their increased prosperity, found the revenue needed to meet increased expenditure.

Hungary became the milch-cow of the Empire. The Austrian provinces, but particularly Vienna, received numerous pledges of Maria Theresa's favour. Compared with their share of the Queen's bounty, that of Hungary was a mere stepchild's portion. But even that was appreciated, and a century after the Queen's death a monument was raised to her memory in the old city of Pozsony. Maria Theresa was the last King (in terms of Hungarian law she was styled King) of the Habsburg line. Her successors, the offspring of her marriage with Francis, Duke of Lorraine, belonged to the Habsburg-Lotharingian dynasty.

COUNT STEPHEN SZÉCHENYI.

(1791—1860)

Maria Theresa's successor. Reign of Joseph II. Hungary and the French Wars. Reforms. National resistance. Count Stephen Széchenyi's youth. Foundation of the Hungarian Academy of Sciences. Széchenyi as a writer. His economic activity. His struggle with Kossuth. Döbling. Széchenyi's achievements. His death.

Maria Theresa's political system did not last as long as her economic scheme. Joseph II (1780—1790) was somewhat parsimonious and disliked pomp and display in the royal household. As King he refused to stand on ceremony. He regarded himself as the first public func-

187

tionary in the land and wished to set a personal example to all his subjects of industry and conscientious attention to duty without any ostentation. The pomp and ceremony of his mother's régime thus came to a sudden end. He had, moreover, a passion for justice. He wished his subjects to enjoy legal equality irrespective of religion or language. In this again he departed from the policy of Maria Theresa who had shown special favour to Catholics and had merely tolerated other denominations. His love of justice, moreover, made him feel the need of bettering the lot of the serfs. He abolished the privileges of the nobles, and taxed all and sundry according to their ability to pay. This, of course, meant a radical reform of the whole political system of the Empire.

From the outset the Emperor realized that his reforms would arouse the antagonism of vested interests, and that it would be impossible to win the assent of the Estates. He therefore decided to govern as an absolute ruler without convoking the Diet. He even refused to be crowned King of Hungary, lest he should be hampered in the realization of his plans by the coronation oath. Many useful and salutary reforms were instituted by his decrees, many of which won general approval. But he went to extremes, which provoked such resistance everywhere that eventually he was obliged to repeal most of his new regulations.

The failure of this attempt to revive absolutism was due to a revival of national sentiment. The rock on which his schemes actually foundered was his proposal to make German the official language in Hungary, on the grounds that Hungarian was unsuitable. The nation was stirred by this affront to a better realization than ever that a race

COUNT STEPHEN SZÉCHENYI

From an engraving by Eugene Doby

LOUIS KOSSUTH

From a drawing by an unknown artist, 1848

lives in its language, and that the danger of losing both tongue and nationality was imminent. From that moment the warnings of George Bessenyei and his comrades of the Life Guards no longer fell on deaf ears. Hungarian national costume and customs became the fashion once again, and national feeling ran as high as in the days of the *Kuruc*. At the same time the more far-seeing among the nobility never lost sight of the need for reforms, and the Diet of 1790—1791 appointed several committees to discuss them and present their reports. It was some decades, however, before anything came of the proposals submitted.

The Diet, like all Europe, was intensely interested in the events that had taken place in Paris. Louis XVI was the brother-in-law of Joseph and his successor Leopold II (1790—1792), and Vienna was far from indifferent to the events in France. There was, furthermore danger of the revolutionary spirit spreading, and in the summer of 1791 Austria and Prussia concluded an alliance. On this becoming known, the French declared war on the allies, and Hungary was dragged into the French wars which lasted from 1792 to 1813, and which cost the country enormous losses in lives, besides ruining it financially.

The excesses of the French Revolution, followed by the Napoleonic régime brought discredit on reform in general all over Europe. Leopold's successor, Francis (1792—1835) would not hear of any change. When the conspiracy of the Abbot Ignatius Martinovics, which aimed at partly realizing the ideas of the French Revolution, failed and its leaders were executed, the King strictly forbade any intellectual movement whatsoever. A strict censorship, a system of spies and secret police controlled the whole country, and none had the courage to take up the cause of reform, the less so because economic conditions were growing more and more difficult, and with increasing destitution the minds of men became more and more pre-occupied with the elementary problem of earning their living.

It was in these lean and cheerless years that the youth of Count Stephen Széchenyi was spent. He was born on 21st September 1791, and there is no cause for wonder if he was haunted throughout his life by the memories of those tragic times. He went into the army, almost as a matter of course, but with Napoleon in exile, he left the service and travelled abroad for several years. His travels were more than mere self-indulgence and amusement. He had an appetite for knowledge and had formed a reso-lution to use the experience gained by foreign travel for the benefit of his country, which had fallen far behind in the general course of progress.

At first he was indifferent to politics, but in 1821—22 the fierce opposition shown by several counties to Imperial decrees levying troops and new taxes impressed and sur-prised him as the demonstration of national energy he had thought entirely dead. From then on he became a keen observer of the trend of events, and when the Government was at last obliged to convoke the Diet in 1825, he decided to enter politics as a member of the Upper House. In the Table of the Magnates, as the Upper Chamber was called, he became the leader of the Opposition. But it was only when he made his appearance in the Lower House that public attention was drawn to him.

Among the subjects that came up from time to time for discussion in Parliament was the cultivation of the

Hungarian language and literature. This subject greatly interested Széchenyi, who, even before the opening of the Diet, had considered the idea of founding some Hungarian learned society, and had made up his mind to a considerable material sacrifice in order to do so. During the session several members expressed a desire to see some such society established, but it was pointed out by Paul Nagy de Felsőbükk, Member for Sopron, that the Commons might merely discuss it and the proposal come to nothing until and unless the Magnates took the matter up and gave it liberal financial support. Reproach of the aristocracy was implied in his speech, and Széchenyi asked to be allowed to say a few words. Few they were, but with them he offered his total income for one year, 60,000 florins, for the purpose of founding a society to promote and encourage Hungarian learning. Széchenyi's speech and his offer made a great impression, and in a short time all the money needed to carry out the scheme was contributed and the Hungarian Academy of Sciences was founded with Széchenyi as its first Vice-President (1831).

He now became one of the leaders in Hungarian public life. Great attention was paid to his speeches and his ideas were universally discussed. He gained much experience. In both Houses he found many honourable and able men, but he also noted the lack of that cohesion among them by means of which their talents and personalities might be put to practical use. The interminable recitation of grievances, the wordy disputes which usually degenerated from empty dialetics to personal insults, were not what he expected of a Diet. He wished to see the spirit of faction ousted from the Chamber and in its place a desire for united action in support of principles. He began by trying to consolidate all the national forces with the object of presenting to the Government a united front based on nationalism. For this purpose he instituted the club system. The first club was founded at Pozsony. In these clubs members of the ruling classes were able to meet regularly and discuss the questions of the moment, so that out of the multiple of individual opinions one or more, generally accepted, emerged. In time these clubs came to play a great part in the social and political life of Hungary, and were centres for the promulgation of progressive ideas and rallying points for parties pursuing a progressive policy.

When Széchenyi's "Credit" was published in 1830, it was eagerly read by a public which hoped to find the exposition of a national programme. In a few months it ran into six editions in the two languages, Hungarian and German. The book fulfilled all expectations. It dealt with Hungary's economic problems. The author pointed out that though the soil of Hungary was rich, the proprietors were poor, the result of a system of agriculture both antiquated and badly organized. There ought to be a better supply of credit, to secure which reform in land-tenure was necessary. The condition of the serfs demanded radical improvement, and trade required the facilities of more and better roads. Free land, free labour and a more equitable system of taxation. These were the ideas contained in "Credit."

The book was a declaration of war on mediaevalism, and caused a great sensation. On the one hand it was intensely popular, on the other, it was fiercely attacked, and its author denounced as a revolutionary bent on upsetting the existing order by violence and endangering the existence of his country. Széchenyi, for his part, had not expected to be universally understood, and to make his intentions clearer he published two other works, "The World" (1831) and "The State" (1833). In the second and more important of the two he set down all the questions that were to come before the Diet when it met. Because of a strict censorship this work had to be circulated in manuscript. Széchenyi's views became the policy of a party calling itself the Liberal Reform Party which acted in Opposition at the Diet of 1832—36.

Széchenyi soon abandoned the arena of party struggles, he was well-acquainted with Prince Metternich and came to the conviction that his programme could not be realized in the near future through political action as the Government was opposed to it. On the other hand he was determined that some way of realizing it should be found. He then proposed that for the present the nation should abandon its political aspirations and concentrate on developing industry and trade. The wealth thus acquired would give it such weight that when it wished to talk politics with Vienna, Vienna would be obliged to listen with respect to what it had to say. This attitude of Széchenyi's brought him into conflict with the other leader of the Liberals, Louis Kossuth, who insisted on laying at least as much stress on political freedom as on economic success.

While Kossuth and his views were growing increasingly popular, Széchenyi pushed on with his plans for economic advancement, confident that they would be justified by events. The regulation of the rivers Danube and Tisza, navigation on the Danube and Lake Balaton, the Chain Bridge and Tunnel in Buda, the canalization of the Iron Gates, etc. were all due to his initiative. It was therefore natural that he became Minister of Transport in the first responsible Hungarian cabinet of the 1848 Parliament. It was furthermore the last public position he ever held. In his reforms England above all was Széchenyi's ideal. He was a disciple of Adam Smith and Bentham. The former had received his father on a visit at his home in Edinburgh (1787); the latter became member of the Hungarian Academy of Sciences.

In the era of reforms — entirely through Széchenyi's influence — such an extraordinary interest was displayed by Hungarians in political and social events in England, in the English language and literature, that an English authoress said that nowhere was Anglomania so much the rage as in Hungary. Frequent manifestations of the great sympathy with England which since then has come to be a national tradition in Hungary are to be found in contemporary books of travel and other literary works.

1848, the year of revolutions, brought Kossuth to the front in Hungary. Széchenyi had never liked Kossuth's revolutionary opinions. He had often attacked them, and when Hungary was driven to take up arms in the defence of her new constitution, he lost his nerve. He reproached himself bitterly for being the prime cause of the bloodshed and misery he foresaw. All his plans, all the results he had been able to achieve were certain, he thought, to be destroyed in the storm that was about to break.

On the verge of a nervous breakdown. Széchenyi retired to an institution for mental diseases at Döbling, near Vienna. There he lived in solitude for several years and when he had once more recovered something of his normal balance he refused to leave Döbling. Yet he continued to take a lively interest in events both at home and abroad. He took up his pen again and in books and pamphlets attacked the new governmental system. As a result the Government put him under strict control. A great sensation was created, however, by the publication in London in 1859 of a book written in German, entitled *"Blick"* ("Review"). Only fifty copies were printed and to-day it is a valuable rarity. In this pamphlet he poured ridicule on the actions of the Austrian Government. He followed the general plan of one of that Government's own publications, *"Rückblick Auf Die Letzten Ereignisse In Ungarn."* ("A review of the latest events in Hungary.") The Government was infuriated by this "review" of their review, and subjected Széchenyi to considerable annoyance in retaliation. He was so badgered and molested that his nervous system again broke down, and worn out by anxiety, he shot himself on the 8th of April, 1860.

Louis Kossuth, his great political antagonist, called Széchenyi "the greatest of Hungarians," and certainly Hungary never had such an apostle to guide and inspire her, or a leader whose ideals and aims were so divorced from self and every class interest. In wisdom, devotion and moderation he was a shining example to all his countrymen. His monument stands in Budapest on the square facing the Academy and close to the Chain Bridge, both of which were of his creation.

LOUIS KOSSUTH.

(1802—1894)

His appearance at the Diet of 1832—36. Activity as journalist. Trial and condemnation. Kossuth and the "Pesti Hirlap." Debate with Széchenyi. Economic action. Kossuth and the Parliament of 1847—48. Kossuth as President of the Committee of National Defence. Preparation for the struggle for independence. Kossuth as Governor of Hungary. Failure. Kossuth in exile. His appearance in Turkey, England and America. Kossuth and the Compromise. Kossuth and the Hungarian people.

Over forty years ago, Louis Kossuth, the maker of modern Hungary, passed away in Turin on March 20th 1894. By that time he had spent almost half a century in exile. Only a few survived in his own country who knew him personally, yet when news of his death arrived the heart of the nation seemed to stand still. The people went into mourning and flocked to the catafalque in the gallery of the National Museum, there to take a final farewell of their great leader. Hundreds of thousands attended the funeral, and there was scarcely a village in the whole country that failed to send a representative. It was as if some magic lingered round his name. He stood for the principle of uncompromising Hungarian independence.

It was at the Diet of 1832—36 that Louis Kossuth (born at Monok 1802) first attracted general attention. Previously he had been prominent in the Country of Zemplén as a fiery advocate of Opposition views and especially of the liberty of the press. It was on that platform in particular that he wished to take his stand in Parliament. He had promised several gentlemen of his country to keep them informed of events in Parliament, which he did in a series of "Parliamentary Reports." The importance of these reports was soon realized by the Liberals, who recognized their value as an ideal means of enlightening the people where politics were concerned. Accordingly they had the originals printed and circulated as widely as possible in Hungary and Transylvania.

No attention was at first paid by the Government to this action of Kossuth. But when it was known that lithographed copies of his writings were being broadcast in numbers he was forbidden to print them. To evade this order, Kossuth again resorted to hand copying. When the Diet closed in 1836, it was Kossuth's intention to continue his chronicle as "Municipal Reports" in which were related the sayings and doings of the local authorities. The Government, however, determined to put a stop to his journalistic activities and forbade their publication. But public opinion was behind Kossuth. The counties, following the example of Pest, openly took his side. The Government then resolved on a bold step and had him arrested for publishing his reports in the face of official prohibition. He was tried for felony and sentenced to four years imprisonment. At the same time Baron Nicholas Wesselényi, one of the most respected members of the Opposition and a popular hero because of his bravery during the Pest floods in 1830, was sentenced to imprisonment along with László Lovassy, the leader of the Hungarian youth.

Kossuth was set at liberty three years later. Captivity had not broken his spirit nor damped his enthusiasm. He was allowed to edit a newspaper which was called the *"Pesti Hirlap"* ("Pest News"). This newspaper was not at first received by the public with marked enthusiasm, but Kossuth was an able editor, and its Opposition spirit soon made it popular. Kossuth was really the founder of Hungarian journalism. He knew how to combine instruction with amusement. His editorials dealt with the important questions of the moment, the activities of the local authorities were reported, political, literary and scientifics events of interest recorded and personal items were not forgotten. It was not long before the new newspaper became a power in the land.

Széchenyi watched the increasing popularity of the *Pesti Hirlap* with anxiety. He disliked its style. For him it was too strident and revolutionary. He feared its effect on the Government would be to set it against any reform whatever, and that his carefully thought-out schemes would be stifled at birth. He then resolved to come out boldy against Kossuth and wrote a book attacking him entitled *"Kelet Népe"* ("People of the East"). It had a mixed reception. Kossuth himself replied to it by pointing out that all the *Pesti Hirlap* had done, and was doing, was to propagate the ideas of Széchenyi himself. The only difference between himself and Széchenyi was one of ends, not of means. "Széchenyi advises us to be wealthy first. Freedom will then not fail to come. I say, Let us first be free, and wealth will not fail to come." Which of them was right might very well still be a matter of dispute.

It was generally held that Kossuth had the best of this exchange of words. Széchenyi himself perhaps felt that he had overshot the mark, and withdrew from politics for a time. At the same time Széchenyi's strictures were not without their effect on Kossuth, who modified the tone of his paper and took more interest in economic development than he had previously done. He set himself to advocate the cause of home industies and when removed from the editor's chair at the instigation of the Viennese authorities, he formed the Hungarian Protective Association for this purpose. He himself was the manager of the association which soon numbered its members in thousands. A great fillip was given to the industrialization of the country. The idea of a railway to Fiume providing Hungarian produce with a direct route to the sea also originated with Kossuth, who saw one of the keys of Hungary's future in maritime trade.

After his retirement from the editorship of the *Pesti Hirlap* Kossuth for some time held aloof from party struggles. The situation had taken a peculiar turn. On the one hand, the Government, which had been consistently opposed to reform of any kind, suddenly changed its tactics, and sought to form a strong Government party for the purpose of carrying out a policy of reform along the lines generally demanded. No great success, however, attended his attempt to make a virtue of what had begun to look like necessity. The Government was much helped at the time by the dissension that had broken out in the liberal ranks over the relations between the local governing bodies and the central authority. One party wanted the hands of the central governing body strengthened at the expense of the counties whereas the other wished the counties to retain all or most of their ancient privileges.

Thus for a long period a shadow hung over the Liberal movement. But in 1847 Francis Deák appeared with proposals which were successful in uniting both parties. A Diet, which promised to be of unique importance in the history of Hungary, was about due to meet, and it was essential that the Reform Party should take its place, solid and united. The Diet met at Pozsony, Kossuth representing the county of Pest. Széchenyi had also a seat in the Lower House.

The discussions dragged on for months without anything of importance resulting, until in February, 1848, the revolution which swept away the French kingdom broke out in Paris. A revolutionary spirit spread all over Europe. Kossuth gave expression to it in a speech that practically urged the Diet to accept the responsibility of making a clean sweep of the obsolete forms of government that were shackling not alone Hungary, but the hereditary provinces of the Empire as well, and to draw up a new and more efficient constitution to replace the old.

The immediate effect of Kossuth's speech was to rouse the population of Vienna, and the Chancellor, Prince Metternich, was expelled from office and compelled to seek safety in flight. When the news of the events in Vienna reached Pest, the youth of that city led by Petőfi, Jókai and Vasvári summed up the national demands under 12 heads which the Municipal Council in Pest was induced to accept. At the same time Kossuth prevailed on the Estates to present an address to the King, calling on him to effect a series of reforms in accordance with the spirit of the times. Ferdinánd V. complied with the petition and agreed to appoint the first responsible Hungarian Cabinet. The leader of the Opposition in the Upper House, Count Batthyány, became Prime Minister. Other ministers were Francis Deák, Kossuth, Széchenyi, Baron Eötvös, all prominent men in political life. On April 11th the laws, which for the greater part had been drafted by Kossuth himself, were ratified by the Emperor. They placed the constitution on an entirely new basis, inasmuch as they introduced a parliament elected by the people, constitutional government, freedom of the press, religious freedom, equality before the law, compulsory taxation for all, and the abolition of serfdom and the privileges of the nobles. With this the ends for which the nation had striven for so long were achieved.

These reforms were not won by revolution but were effected by the joint will of King and people. They were legally established. Thanks to them the free population of Hungary was increased overnight by many millions through the emancipation of the serfs of all nationalities, Slovaks, Germans, Serbs, and Wallachians, as well as Magyars. No discrimination was made as to language or nationality. Magyar nobles had to part with the sole right to freehold property which had now been acquired by liberated serfs even of other races. This generous policy should have proved a corrective to the separatist tendencies previously encouraged by Vienna. But after these legislative measures had obtained royal sanction intrigue was as busy as ever in its efforts to rouse the nationalities against them and against the new order inaugurated by them, for the economic jealousy of Austria had been aroused. Arms and money were distributed and in a few weeks there was open revolt in several districts against the constitutional government.

The first representative Parliament took steps to meet this danger by authorizing the formation of a national army. The proposal came from Kossuth and was unanimously approved. Thus arose the army of *Honvéds* (National Defence).

Thereafter events moved rapidly. With the compliance of the Vienna Government, the Ban of Croatia, Jellachich, invaded Hungary. The Prime Minister endeavoured to dissuade him from this step, but in vain. When it was certain beyond doubt that Jellachich was backed by Vienna, the Hungarian Cabinet resigned, and Parliament appointed a Committee of National Defence and entrusted it with the government of the country. Kossuth, the heart and soul of the movement, became President and prepared for armed conflict. The army had to be swiftly organized, and to aid the speed-up in recruiting, Kossuth made a tour of the most important towns of the Great Plain. His eloquance drew thousands to enlist in defence of their "sacred freedom." An army was soon conjured into existence which quickly cleared the country of Jellachich and his followers and put down further attempts at revolt.

At this stage the Austrian Government intervened. It was alleged that the Vienna rising had been engineered by Hungarians and that Hungarian forces had crossed the Austrian frontier to support it. General Windischgrætz was despatched to Hungary at the head of a large army with orders "to tidy up." He defeated the raw *Honvéd* regiments in several engagements and entered Buda in

January, 1849. The governing Committee had previously moved to Debrecen, from whence the organizing of national resistance was being directed.

Kossuth made good use of the respite afforded him by the winter. He brought an energy that seemed almost superhuman to the reorganization of the *Honvéds*, put financial matters to right, saw to it that local administration was efficient, tentatively entered into negotiations with foreign powers and above all inspired the country with a faith in final victory. The *Honvéd* troops under the command of Görgey, Damjanich, Klapka, and of Bem in Transylvania, not only justified, but even surpassed all expectations. When they began to counter-attack in the spring, the greater part of the country was in the hands of the enemy. By the end cf May the *Honvéds* had retaken all Hungary. It was a triumphant campaign of victory after victory, and on 21st May they even took the fortress of Buda.

The Austrian Government could not acquiesce in such a series of disgraceful defeats. A further excuse to continue hostilities was afforded by the Hungarian Parliament assembled at Debrecen, which formally dethroned the Habsburgs and declared Hungary independent. The Imperial Government was spurred on by more than mere wounded pride to crush Kossuth and his people. But Vienna did not feel equal to attempting this alone and solicited the aid of the Tsar. Nicholas, a fanatic in his hatred of all revolutions, gladly agreed to supply the help required. The odds against Hungary then became hopeless and even Kossuth despaired of being able to fight successfully against them. Consequently he resigned office as Governor, handed over the direction of affairs to

Arthur Görgey, the commander-in-chief of the *Honvéd* army, and left the country. Görgey realizing that further resistance was hopeless, surrendered to the Russians at Világos on August 13th 1849. Thus ended the Hungarian War of Independence. Kossuth fled first to Turkey and then in 1851 to England, where he began a great propaganda campaign calculated to enlighten foreign opinion concerning the situation in Hungary. The English people received him as the heroic champion of human rights, and wherever he spoke he was received with acclamation. Both in England and the United States, where Kossuth also passed a few months, the Hungarian question became one of the topics of the day. On both sides of the Atlantic Kossuth came to be regarded as an apostle of national freedom and human rights. In exile he became an important factor in European politics, always working for one end, an independent Hungary. Both Napoleon III and the Italians were induced to support Hungarian aspirations, at least so far as expressions of sympathy went. In actual practice, however, Zrinyi's saying that we could rely on no one but ourselves was once again endorsed by history.

Kossuth, however, did not relax his effort in the face of more than one failure. He followed the trend of European events attentively, and whenever conditions seemed favourable, he pressed Hungary's case. It was only after the compromise of 1867 that he ceased his diplomatic activities. He himself was opposed to the compromise, but did not wish by impolitic interference to hinder the development of Hungary which was then beginning. He loved his country as a man and a Hungarian and not as a *doctrinaire* of political principles. In 1863 he made his home in Turin and from thence watched with interest and affection the course of events in his native land. Nothing that happened there escaped his notice. Ultimately, he came to be regarded as a national prophet whose words were listened to even by men with entirely different political views. His modest home became a place of pilgrimage for all who shared his ambitions for Hungary. No name is more highly revered in Hungary than his. To the day of his death, which took place at Turin on March 20th 1894 he was the uncrowned king of his country, and even to-day his work is in no danger of being forgotten.

FRANCIS DEÁK.

(1803—1876)

Deák at the Diets of 1832—36 and 1839—40. The problem of taxation and the knights of the shires. Deák withdraws from political life. Minister of Justice in the Cabinet of 1848. His resignation. His part during the period of absolutism and at the diet of 1861. Two addresses. The Easter paragraph. The compromise of 1867.

When Anthony Deák, who represented the County of Zala at the Diet of 1832—36, retired from political life, he remarked to those friends who tried to dissuade him: "I'll send you a young man who has more in his little finger than I have in my whole body." The young man in question turned out to be a kinsman, Francis Deák (Born 17th October, 1803), who was acting-governor of the County of Zala and whose legal knowledge and acumen were recognised all over the country.

There was no lack of able men in the Liberal Party at that time, and it was not easy for Deák to make a mark for himself, but his speeches on the question of the emancipation of the serfs attracted public attention. It was obvious that here was a man well-versed in the history of his country as only too few were. The Diet of 1839—40 saw him already as one of the leaders of the Liberal opposition.

To checkmate the reform movement led by Kossuth the Government sought to control members of the Diet through the country authorities, whose instructions they were obliged to follow. There were many squires who were opposed to measures that robbed them of privileges they had always enjoyed. Before the Diet of 1843—1844 "no tax-paying" had become the slogan of a large party of squires all over the country. It was the same in Zala, Deák's own county. There the majority voted against paying taxes, whereupon Deák refused to accept the mandate. The County of Pest, the one with the greatest prestige in the country, offered to find him a seat, but he was firm in his resolution to hold aloof. His absence was felt in a Diet concerned with many measures on which he could have spoken with authority. Indeed, the Diet of Pozsony (1843—44) was totally lacking in leadership, for Széchenyi was in the Upper House and Kossuth was not a member.

When the Diet of '47 met, Deák was ill, but upon Count Batthyány being made Prime Minister, he offered Deák the Portfolio of Justice. It was accepted and thereafter he stood for moderate views in the Cabinet against the extremists. Outside his office he had little to do with the control of public opinion. His cool head and matter-of-fact way of looking at things were less adapted to the

FRANCIS JOSEPH I

From an engraving executed in 185

ELIZABETH, QUEEN OF HUNGARY

From a contemporary engraving

temper of the times than Kossuth's fiery personality. He applied himself to the preparation of those legal reforms which were so urgently demanded by changed circumstances in the whole national life. Upon the resignation of the Batthyány Ministry, Deák practically ceased to take any part in public affairs.

He did not follow Kossuth and the Diet to Debrecen. During the tragic events of the War of Independence he lived quietly on his estate at Kehida. He was naturally much moved to hear of the atrocities committed by the vengeful Austrians, but he kept his head, trusting that time was on the side of justice and of Hungary. People came to look to him for advice, and he always counselled patience.

He moved to Pest in '54, and his modest apartment in "The Queen of England" hotel became the nerve centre of Hungarian politics. Hope was languishing in those days in Hungary. Men preferred to let their minds rest on the past rather than dwell on the future. Under the pressure of a hateful absolutism Hungarian national feeling was strengthened and there came a day when Vienna could no longer afford to ignore it.

In 1860 an Imperial decree granted a constitution to the constituent parts of the Habsburg Empire, Hungary included. This *"Diploma,"* as it was called, completely ignored the past, and there was nothing in it to indicate that a Hungarian Parliament or a Hungarian constitution had ever existed. It merely re-established the old Diet, stripped, however, of any power to deal with military, financial or commercial questions. These were handed over to an Imperial Council in which, it is true, Hungary might be represented.

The *"Diploma"* was certainly an advance on the despotic attitude hitherto adopted, but it was at variance with the constitution of '48 and in Deák's view quite unacceptable. He advised the Emperor to re-establish the Hungarian constitution, assuring him that once in being a Hungarian Parliament would be reasonable and ready to come to an understanding in matters affecting relations with the Empire.

This counsel was not acted on at the time and the Diet as constituted by the decree met in '61. Two views were represented at the assembly. One party, led by Count László Teleki who had just returned from exile, urged that there should be no dealing with the throne on the basis of the decrees, and moved that the Diet should protest and dissolve. These "Resolutionists," as they were called, were in the majority. In opposition to this stood Deák, who pleaded for a less obstinate attitude, and urged the Diet to give full expression to its views in an Address to the Emperor, in the hope of at least partially saving the situation.

When Teleki's health broke down in '61 and he committed suicide, the Resolutionists began to lose ground, and eventually Deák's advice was accepted. He prepared the Address and presented it to the Emperor.

It was a masterly *exposé* of the Hungarian constitution, and made a deep and lasting impression when published. At the Vienna Court, however, the Emperor and his advisers had hardened their hearts and declaring that after the events of '48—'49, an autonomous Hungary was out of the question, returned the Address.

When the Address came back with the notes appended Deák and his colleagues discussed the situation and resolved to send another. This was also prepared by Deák, and it left no doubt that on the Hungarian side there was to be no bargaining over the Hungarian Constitution. "The Hungarian people will endure as their ancestors endured and suffered in their struggle to preserve the rights of their country. What we have lost through violence and force time and fate may restore, but the recovery by a nation of what has been resigned through fear of suffering is always difficult and doubtful."

Following the second Address, the Diet was dissoved (1861). It was a sign of an altered view of the situation that the rejection of the Address was calmly received. The feeling was abroad that the days of absolutism were numbered, and that the nation could afford to be patient.

While constitutional activity was suspended, Deák resumed his life of retirement and watchfulness. It was at this time that he wrote his "Contribution to Hungarian Public Law," which even to-day is the standard work on the subject.

Patience had its reward. Before long it became known that the Emperor would welcome overtures towards a compromise on the part of the Hungarians. Deák therupon published an unsigned article in the "*Pesti Napló*," tactfully suggesting that by an act of magnanimity the Emperor could do much to reconcile his Hungarian subjects. The hand thus offered was taken by Francis Joseph. He made a gift from the Privy Purse to the Hungarian Academy, came to Pest to meet the Hungarian leaders, and finally convoked the Diet in 1865. With this move negotiations began in earnest, and ultimately an agreement was reached in 1867. The result was that the Hungarian constitution was re-established on the lines of the laws of 1848, and the relations between Hungary and Austria defined in the Pragmatic Sanction. A Cabinet was appointed with Count Julius Andrássy as Prime Minister, and Francis Joseph and his consort were crowned King and Queen of Hungary. With this ceremony, Hungarian autonomy was formally acknowledged.

The Compromise of 1867 was Deák's greatest achievement. By this he rendered a great service, not only to Hungary but also to the Empire of the Habsburgs, henceforth styled Austria-Hungary. Gladstone on introducing his first Home Rule Bill in the British House of Commons quoted the Compromise and its effects to justify his own measure. The parallel was not as true as he imagined it to be but he was right when he pointed to the salutary effects that resulted from it, and because of it the Empire acquired a new prestige and importance.

Satisfactory as the Compromise was for the time being, Deák did not consider that it settled the relation between Austria and Hungary in the long run. It was a compromise and contained unreconciled elements. The important thing about it, however, was that it secured temporarily the political stability necessary as a basis for internal development and progress. Naturally there were some who did not take kindly to the concessions made in the Compromise and a party formed itself round Kálmán Tisza in opposition to Deák, which held out for the complete endorsement of the laws of 1848, while another again demanded complete separation from Austria. In the years succeeding the Compromise, however, Deák's party was easily the more influential, largely owing to the able leadership of Count Andrássy.

FRANCIS DEÁK

From an engraving executed in 1866 by Joseph Marastoni

COUNT JULIUS ANDRÁSSY

From an engraving executed in 1861 by Joseph Marastoni

Count Julius Andrássy had taken a prominent part in the Revolution, and on its collapse had found refuge in England and France. While in England he found that though wide-spread sympathy existed for the ideas of the Hungarian revolutionaries, the political leaders would not hear of the destruction of the Habsburg Empire. He came to the view that if the Hungarians pressed the claims of nationalism too far, they might end in being isolated in the midst of the much greater national movements going on round them and find themselves powerless to maintain their hold on their own country in face of the demands of the national minorities within its borders, and returned to Hungary convinced that it was in its true interest to preserve the link with the Empire.

As Prime Minister, accordingly, he was a whole-hearted supporter of the Compromise. In his opinion it gave Hungary all she really needed. Many problems affecting the material well-being of the people were in urgent need of attention, and Andrássy was not inclined to split hairs on constitutional questions while these remained unsolved.

While he remained at the helm, his party kept its majority in the country, but on his transfer to Vienna as Foreign Minister, the tide of public opinion turned. Deák was aging and no other outstanding personality rose as leader. Ultimately the government was taken over by a new party formed by an amalgamation of Deák's Party with the Left Centre led by Coloman Tisza. This new body accepted the Compromise, and remained in power for thirty years. During this long period, three outstanding men rose to the surface on the current of events: Coloman Tisza, Alexander Wekerle and Stephen Tisza, Coloman's son.

Coloman Tisza continued the policy of Andrássy. Without being enthusiastic for the Compromise, he nevertheless realized that the general situation made it a necessity for the time being. On all sides there was unrest, and storms frequently burst in the Balkans. Internal solidarity was therefore more essential than ever. He determined to leave the legal question of the relations between Hungary and Austria alone and concentrate his efforts on economic development.

One element of the Compromise had, however, dangerous possibilities. Military organization had been left pretty much untouched. The army, whose officers were mostly of Slav origin, remained as it had been before 1867, inbued with the spirit of centralism. Between the army and the people there was open antagonism, which led to frequent "incidents," and finally to the overthrow of the Tisza Cabinet.

Great things were achieved in the sphere of trade and finance by Alexander Wekerle, Minister of Finance and later Prime Minister. Hungarian currency came to rank with the best in Europe, and at the National Exhibition of 1896, which was held to celebrate the thousandth anniversary of the settlement of the Hungarians in their country, the whole world was given splendid evidence of Hungary's development.

But along with economic advance went political decay. The feeling of dissatisfaction with the Compromise grew apace. Parliament became the scene of many disturbances. The Opposition seized on the character of the army as the most favourable point of attack on the Government. The army was unpopular because it was foreign and used a foreign language, German. Accordingly, when men and supplies were asked for in 1902, though the situation warranted the demand it was vehemently opposed. The public sided with the Opposition, all the more strongly when their nationalism was further intensified by the cry that Hungary should be made an autonomous customs area.

Francis Joseph was bitterly opposed to those disruptive movements as he considered them, and at this time the gulf between him and his Hungarian subjects grew very wide indeed.

None realized how deplorable this was more acutely than Stephen Tisza, who formed his first Cabinet in 1903. He had been a Member of Parliament since 1887 and had had abundant opportunities of seeing how the unyielding temper of the Emperor on the one hand, and the revolutionary spirit of the extremists on the other, were leading to a complete *impasse*. He himself supported the Compromise. He was a man of deep national feeling, but he stood firmly for union with Austria. The best interests of Hungary demanded the existence of a strong and united Austria-Hungary. Only within Austria-Hungary could the racially isolated Hungarians retain secure possession of their lands against the encroachments of the Slavs, the Wallachians and the Germans. This constituted Tisza's fundamental outlook.

Again Tisza saw clearly that in a trial of strength Hungary would be at a disadvantage compared with Austria, for in all military and economic questions all parties and sections in Austria were united in their opposition to Hungary, whereas Hungary could not rely on the support of her varied nationalities. These nationalities, who in the course of centuries had settled within the borders of Hungary, had remained unassimilated, and they were always found to be willing tools of the central Imperial authorities against the Hungarian nationalist movement. As long as there remained such an economic and cultural disparity between the two partners, Tisza considered that any serious anti-Austrian movement would be injurious to Hungary.

He therefore stood for the Compromise and further for parliamentary reform. He was anxious to raise the standard of parliamentary efficiency, to cut out the petty quarrels and personal enmities over which so much time was wasted, and to regulate procedure to make parliamentary action less dilatory and more effective. But his reforms did not meet with a good reception, and his party was defeated in 1905 upon which he resigned. Four years later it was again returned to power, and the reforms were carried through.

Tisza was Prime Minister when the World War broke out in 1914. The question has been raised whether he was in any way responsible.

When Tisza heard of the murder of the Archduke Ferdinand, he was at first, like so many people, incredulous and then deeply shocked. That it might lead to a general conflagration did not occur to him. It was only when he met Count Berchtold in Vienna that he realized that the then Foreign Minister wished to take advantage of "the Sarajevo outrage to settle accounts with Serbia." Count Berchtold's remark surprised him, and he let it be known that he considered the Foreign Minister's projected step a "fatal mistake," and that he would not share the responsibility for it. He expressed his misgivings in a special memorandum presented to the Emperor at the beginning of July.

At the meeting of the Cabinet held on the 7th of that month, he stuck to his opinion. He said he could never agree to a sudden attack on Serbia delivered without regular diplomatic preliminaries. At this protest the idea of a surprise attack was dropped, but all agreed, with the single exception of Tisza, that to punish Serbia for her obvious complicity in the Archduke's assassination, demands such as she would be morally incapable of accepting, should be made of her. Tisza was opposed to this ; he agreed that the case merited severe conditions being attached to any demand for satisfaction, but said they should be within the bounds of reason. He again expressed his views on the following day in an official report which he presented to the Emperor, in which he stated that he could not fall in with what was proposed by the other members of the Council. He directed the Emperor's attention to the cost of a war, and finally declared himself "after most scrupulous consideration to be unable to share the responsibility for an attack on Serbia."

Tisza took pains to point out in his report of July 8th that there should at any rate be no question of the annihilation or annexation of Serbia, and that if Serbia gave way Austria-Hungary must be content. On July 9th Tisza informed his colleagues in the Hungarian Cabinet of his attitude, which was approved by them.

From this it is obvious that of all those holding responsible office in the Austro-Hungarian Government before the outbreak of war, Count Tisza, representing Hungary, alone opposed war and worked for a peaceful settlement. It was regrettable that the Serb press adopted an extremely bellicose attitude and did its utmost to exacerbate national feelings on both sides. It was then well known in Imperial diplomatic circles and has since come to be acknowledged in all well informed quarters in Great Britain that the assassination was connived at by the Serbian Government, which was furthermore the guiding hand behind the Serb press campaign. On the other hand, Austria-Hungary could not aquiesce in continued dilatoriness without severe loss of prestige, nor could she find any sound excuse for it. Eventually she was obliged to resort to a threat of force, and things reached the ultimatum stage. Tisza still pressed for less obstinacy, and was so far successful as to obtain a statement to the effect that Austria-Hungary was not animated by an intention to deprive Serbia of territory.

The tone of the ultimatum was severe but its terms were not impossible. Tisza had consented to it because he thought Serbia could comply with its demands without feeling unduly humiliated. He expected an answer that would lead to further negotiations and declared in the House on the 24th July: "We are seeking peace and desire peace." Serbia did not, however, accept the terms of the ultimatum and thus the World War began.

Tisza remained silent about his opposition to the course that led to war, and later when the Left sought to cover him with obloquy as one of the authors of the war he uttered not a word. He cared nothing for popularity, and disdained to make use of the ordinary stratagems of the popular politician, either to win sympathy or to avoid public execration. He was a Calvinist and held that it was preordained by Providence that he was to be Prime

COUNT STEPHEN TISZA

Photograph by Szenes, successor to Professor Koller

CHARLES IV WITH QUEEN ZITA AND PRINCE OTTO

Photograph by Béla Halmi

Minister at the outbreak of the war and consequently he had to accept the full weight of responsibility. This religious feeling explains the apparent contradiction in his conduct by remaining in office during a war to which he had been bitterly opposed. Another, and a strong reason for his remaining in office was that the aged Emperor had himself explicity asked Tisza to stand by him in the time of trial, and this request from such a quarter appealed with all the force of an obligation to a man of Count Tisza's stamp.

His published letters show how much he accomplished during the first years of the war. Of special interest was his attempt to solve the racial problems in Hungary. He had intimate knowledge of these problems since his ancestral estates were situated in districts where there was a large non-Magyar population. He believed that the cultural aspirations of these racial minorities could be satisfied without ruining the political fabric of Hungary. He had begun negotiations with the leaders of the nationalities before the outbreak of war, and continued them after hostilities had commenced. His efforts were foiled through the lack of sincerity on the part of the nationalities. They merely manœuvred with Tisza while remaining in touch with their fellow racials over the frontier. Any agreement they made was made with mental reservations that rendered it abortive. It is not to be wondered at that Tisza could do nothing with them.

Francis Joseph's death meant the end of Stephen Tisza's political career. The Emperor Charles disliked him. Tisza's personality was too dominating for him, and in the summer of 1917, Tisza resigned. From that time on he was either at the front or living in retirement.

When he saw collapse impending, he thought of returning to active service. His party was still intact, and though he had become unpopular with the people as a whole, it was thought that his strong character and intelligence might be able to check the rot that had set in. Alas, it was not to be. Four criminals entered his house and under the plea that they had come to strike down the author of the war, murdered him. (31 Oct. 1918.)

The flood of the revolution followed. It was led by a highly incompetent individual of less than doubtful morals and it effectively ruined this millenarian kingdom, preparing, as it did the way for Bolshevism, which in 1919 laid the country waste for four and a half months. What the World War had left Bolshevism destroyed. Hungary, impotent, was exposed to the rapacity of her neighbours, who stripped her of nearly three-quarters of her territory. The Great Powers, ignorant of the conditions prevailing in this part of Europe, sanctioned the new frontiers in the Treaty of Trianon.

Count Tisza, in one of his political essays wrote as follows: "The destiny of Man does not depend on mere chance. The ship of humanity is not tossed about by the caprice of a blind fate. A wise hand steers her through the reefs and rocks of trials, suffering and bloodshed forward to her great goal."

And that remains the historical philosophy held by Trianon Hungary.

INDEX

KINGS OF HUNGARY

St. Stephen 997—1038
Peter 1038—41 and 1044—1047
Samuel Aba 1041—1044
Andrew I. 1047—1060
Béla I. 1060—1063
Salamon 1063—1074
Géza I. 1074—1077
St. Ladislas 1077—1095
Coloman 1095—1116
Stephen II. 1116—1131
Béla II. 1131—1141
Géza II. 1141—1161
Stephen III. 1161—1172
Ladislas II. 1161—1162
Stephen IV. 1162—1163
Béla III. 1173—1196
Emery 1196—1204
Ladislas III. 1204—1205
Andrew II. 1205—1235
Béla IV. 1235—1270
Stephen V. 1270—1272
Ladislas IV. 1272—1290
Andrew III. 1290—1301
Wenceslas 1301—1304
Otto 1305—1308
Robert Charles 1308—1342
Louis The Great 1342—1382

Maria 1382—1395
Charles II. 1385
Sigismund 1395—1437
Albert 1437—1439
Wladislas I. 1440—1444
Ladislas V. 1445—1457
Mathias I. 1458—1490
Wladislas II. 1490—1516
Louis II. 1516—1526
John Szapolyai 1526—1540
Ferdinand I. 1526—1564
Maximilian 1564—1576
Rudolph 1576—1608
Mathias II. 1608—1619
Ferdinand II. 1619—1637
Ferdinand III. 1637—1657
Ferdinand IV.
Leopold I. 1657—1705
Joseph I. 1705—1711
Charles III. 1711—1740
Maria Theresa 1740—1780
Joseph II. 1780—1790
Leopold II. 1790—1792
Francis 1792—1835
Ferdinand V. 1835—1848
Francis Joseph 1848—1916
Charles IV. 1916—1918

PRINCES OF TRANSYLVANIA

John Sigismund 1540—1571
Stephen Báthory 1571—1576
Christopher Báthory 1576—1581
Sigismund Báthory 1581—1598 and
    1600—1601
Andrew Báthory 1598—1599
Moses Székely 1603
Stephen Bocskay 1605—1606
Sigismund Rákóczi 1606—1608
Gabriel Báthory 1608—1613
Gabriel Bethlen 1613—1629
Catherine 1629—1630

Stephen Bethlen 1630
George Rákóczi I. 1630—1648
George Rákóczi II. 1648—1660
Francis Rákóczi I. — —
Francis Rhédey 1657—1658
Ákos Barcsay 1658—1660
John Kemény 1661—1662
Michael Apafi I. 1662—1690
Michael Apafi II. 1690
Emery Thököly 1690
Francis Rákóczi II. 1705—1711